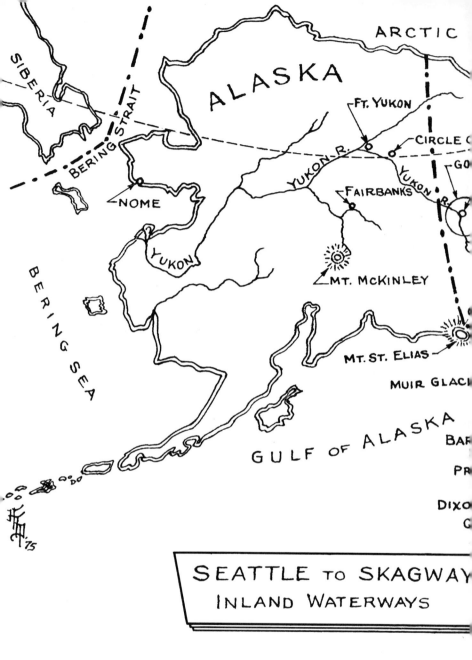

SEATTLE TO SKAGWAY
INLAND WATERWAYS

THIS BOOK
IS OF BICENTENNIAL INTEREST

The old Ball homestead, a tract of 212 acres, was awarded to Daniel Murray, an uncle of the Balls, for his services in the Revolutionary War. This land, watered by 26 springs, was farmed by the Balls for about 140 years. A. E. Ball, in his later years, replanted thousands of walnut, pine and maple trees on it to replace the ones he as a boy had helped cut down to clear the fields for farming.

At the turn of the century an organization was formed by the Descendents of the Signers of the Declaration of Independence, of which Amos Entheus Ball was a charter member. His father, Amos Walton Ball, was descended from George Walton, who signed for Georgia.

As a coincidence, in the Klondike episode where A. E. Ball carried the Widow Purdy across the flooded stream, it was later found that she was descended from Button Gwinnett, also a signer of the Declaration of Independence from Georgia.

And so the pioneer spirit rolls on.

TENDERFOOT TO SOURDOUGH

The True Adventures of

AMOS ENTHEUS BALL
in the
KLONDIKE GOLD RUSH
as told in his own words

by Hazel T. Procter

NEW HOLLAND, PENNSYLVANIA

Edward C. Procter - Printer

1975

Published by Edward C. Procter, CUSTOM PRINTING
210 Hillcrest Road New Holland, Pennsylvania 17557

DEDICATED TO THE GRANDPARENTS—
              PIONEERS OF THE PAST

AND TO OUR GRANDCHILDREN—
              PIONEERS OF THE FUTURE

AND TO FAITHFUL CHILDREN WHO MAKE
              POSSIBLE A BETTER PRESENT

CONTENTS

TENDERFOOT TO SOURDOUGH

PICTURES and MAPS

Totem Pole Picture, Queen Liliuokalani Illustration, and sketches
illustrating the chapters were drawn by Edward C. Procter.

Foreword

A generation has passed since the 20th century was ushered in with one of the most bizarre episodes in the history of the American continent—the Klondike Gold Rush. The discovery of gold in Canada's Yukon Territory by Robert Henderson and George Carmack was a magnet that drew hundreds of thousands of adventurers from all over the world and from all stations of life to this bleak and forbidding 'moose pasture' to suffer all manner of hardship for the lure of gold and the riches it promised.

Children growing up around 1896–1904 usually had heard first hand tales from some uncle or neighbor or friend who had braved that frozen land to search for the precious metal. For the children whose father had come back alive from such a rugged adventure, the Klondike Gold Rush lived and their father was a local hero, looked up to by all who knew him. Such a man was asked many times to speak before the local schools, to tell first hand the rigors of life in this wilderness of ice and snow, battling with starvation, wild beasts and the ever freezing cold. Then there were treasures other than gold that the Klondikers brought home: bones of the extinct mastodon and many other animals buried mountain deep for millions of years; there were gem stones of garnets, agates, black diamonds and gold nuggets to make children's eyes pop with wonder. But the tales of courage and endurance for the hope of discovery of the riches of this new land were sought and listened to with awe by young and old alike.

Today that whole era of discovery and the wild rush for gold which lived so vividly for the children of the early 1900's is now vaguely condensed into a few lines in our history books. The average youth of today scarcely knows there was such an exciting chapter in the history of America, and that it was followed by the discovery of gold for our own country in Alaska. A number of books have been written giving the entire history of the Gold Rush with its fantastic venturers. But out of it all there emerged a few thousand level headed pioneers, undismayed by hardship, who 'slugged it out' on foot over the mountains, down the tempestuous waterways, and on to the Klondike. Here they patiently thawed the earth and picked and dug until they found the treasured metal.

This is to preserve for our children just one account of what the Gold Rush was like and the fortitude required to be a pioneer.

The adventures in this book, briefed in his diary and memoirs, really happened and furnished the tales this father never tired of telling to the many people who visited the old homestead to hear them, and to see the curious treasures of earth he had brought home from his gold mine in the Klondike.

Illustrated and told in his own words by his daughter —

Hazel T. Procter

ACKNOWLEDGMENTS

To my father, Amos Entheus Ball, for his daily diary of these rugged events as they happened during his three years in the Klondike Gold Rush. After his return home, on winter evenings, Father's diary was amplified by his many memoirs recalled and dictated to my mother to transcribe as we all sat around the warmth of the living room heater and listened.

Many times it was also with others present. We heard these tales told hundreds of times to relatives, friends, or classes from various schools. The authenticity of it all was always illustrated by examining the many curios brought from his gold mine: mastodon teeth and part of an ivory tusk, gold dust and nuggets, garnets, black diamonds, and dozens of other fossils and items from his large cabinet, together with photographs of the whole Gold Rush area.

These many transcripts of Father's experiences, in both his own and Mother's handwriting, had become brittle with age and could have been lost but for Mother's love and care for them. To preclude such a loss and preserve for all the original content of Father's memoirs is the purpose of this book.

An especial acknowledgement of thanks is due my friend, Charles F. Hamilton, whose experience as a young author he shared to help with the procedure required.

Gratitude is also due to my family and a number of friends, including Lancaster artist, Florence Starr Taylor, for their honest criticism and encouragement of this work; and especially to my son, Edward C. Procter, for inking my illustrations and maps, sketching the chapter illustrations, and for printing the book.

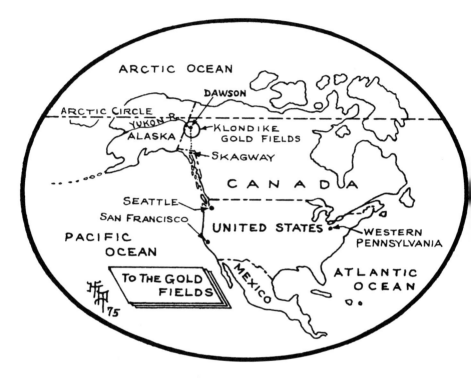

ARCTIC OCEAN

DAWSON

ARCTIC CIRCLE

YUKON R.

ALASKA

KLONDIKE
GOLD FIELDS

SKAGWAY

C A N A D A

SEATTLE

SAN FRANCISCO

PACIFIC
OCEAN

UNITED STATES

WESTERN
PENNSYLVANIA

TO THE GOLD
FIELDS

MEXICO

ATLANTIC
OCEAN

75

TENDERFOOT TO SOURDOUGH

The True Adventures of Amos Entheus Ball in the Klondike Gold Rush as told in his own words

———————— ◇ ————————

* * * * CHAPTER 1 * * * *

Debts vs Grit

"Entheus, come with me," I read. "This is the opportunity of a lifetime! You will plod along on that farm for the rest of your life before you get its cost paid off. You might strike it rich in the Klondike and have it all free of debt in about a year." That was brother Kinsley out in Seattle, trying to urge me to strike out with him to the gold fields around Dawson in 1900. Sure! He had made money in real estate. Seattle was booming. He had money for outfits and to stake a claim. All I had was debts; then being double crossed and more debts.

When Father died in 1890 he had called me to his bedside. "Promise me you will take over the old farm homestead and keep it in the family" he begged. It was home and I loved it too. Hadn't my circuit riding preacher grandfather pioneered here in western Pennsylvania and built his log house sixty feet long so he could call the early settlers to meet in his home for church and teach their young ones to live by the word of God. And then next the orchard the old graveyard he had made to bury all their dead,—and all the Balls,—even his grandfather Zopher Ball who had struck up north from Virginia, where,—cousin kin,— they had neighbored with the Washingtons. Yes I had taken over the old home but I had all my brothers' and sisters' shares to pay off, besides my mother's dowery each year so long as she lived. My brothers numbered a doctor, a dentist and surgeon, a real estate broker, a livery stable operator, and a professor who later became a lawyer; while the girls had taught school and nursed. I was the only one who loved the land and its history enough to save it as our home.

The neighbors all plied me with their fears. "You'd never come back alive from that awful cold country." "I hear tell it gets down to 75° below zero up there so near the North Pole." "You wouldn't ketch me goin' way off up there!" Still the offer did sound enticing,—like one grand adventure,—and I loved that. Maybe I could start all over again with my life and win. But I still needed money and would have to borrow again even to go. I was not one to jump blindly into an unknown thing without considering it carefully. Here I was in my prime and old enough to have practical experience. Father had taught me to plow at 10, then I had helped him tear down the old log barn and build one new and large, all frame. That developed muscle and skill. But at 17 I did the work of a man and helped Father make the brick and build our new ten room house in 1875. All this was part of growing up; but my best training came from my faithful little mother who instilled a love of good principles whereby to honor a worthy heritage. When I was 12 she asked me to be a good example to all my younger brothers and said, "I want you to promise me, Entheus, never to smoke, chew tobacco, or drink intoxicant liquors, but keep good morals and be truthful and honest in all you do". That gave real strength and needed courage.

Right now I needed all the courage I could command. We had no bank in our small town at this time, so in money matters we had to help each other. One of the neighbors told me of an old man in the next county who sometimes had money to lend. "He'll put you through the 33rd degree though before you get it. He's not one to take chances." So I made bold to go see him. "Well, lad, you need money? Let's see if you're worth it and know how to use it. I want this money back one day you know. Tell me about yourself." And he leaned back in his chair to listen.

"Well," I began, "I fully respect your position and can tell you I'm a hard worker and an honest one, and I know what it is to go through hard times and get along with what you have." "Give me an example," he urged. "Did you get much schooling?" "Our mother was a teacher. Beyond common school, my older sister and I had two terms at Edinboro State Normal. But just then our country was stricken with the money panic of the later 1870's. Money was so scarce that wages could not be had at any price." "So what did you do? I well remember those days." And the old man leaned forward. "My grand uncle in Indiana needed help on his large farm," I continued, "so I walked through—a distance of 350 miles. Farm produce was so low that butter brought only six to eight cents a pound in trade; eggs were four cents a dozen; corn, seven cents a bushel; fat hogs—" The old man's eyes flashed as he interrupted, "I sold mine for only three cents a pound,—and that was dressed! My best cows brought $12 to $15 dollars. Farm wages only 50¢ a day,—Aye! don't I remember! And clothing was homespun and made at home! You've been through it lad! What else did you do?"

I told him then about my uncle's sick nephew, and how I had walked a mile and a half every other night to care for him for seven months with no recompense, and all the while worked full time on the farm by day. "Aye! but lad, you were recompensed! You were building endurance and patience and compassion. But now what about the money you earned on the uncle's farm? Did you spend it?" "Not when I earned it so hard—not I. At the end of two years I had saved most every cent, so went back home, bought a small acreage nearby and farmed it."

"Were you ever in trouble—deep trouble?" the old man probed. "Well, yes; in December 1886 I had a rugged experience. I had contracted to haul some new iron bridges to span Deer Creek. It began to rain and turned into a torrent of storm which washed the temporary bridge away, so I had to ride one mare across the turbulent stream, three feet deep and raging. Midway the mare slipped and fell and the rushing water rolled us over and over before we could struggle out. I had then quickly hitched to the wagon, poured the water out of my boots and made the team run to get warm. My clothes were frozen stiff, but we kept running for it was turning very cold and icy. We had 10 more miles to go with many rest stops, but I finally got the team and wagon home about midnight. With the team cared for in the barn and blanketed, I had stumbled half frozen to the house, only to find the door locked with the key at the neighbors. At last I got into the house, built a fire in the stove and got dry clothes and warmed; then with a lunch, refreshed but weary, I had got to bed about 2 A.M." From an inner pocket, I pulled out my diary with the hope it might convince of my worthiness. Here's what I wrote after I thawed out from that experience. "I feel thankful, for this might have been worse. It is such experiences that test the quality of a man and make him more capable of succeeding when sore trials come his way."

"Gumption! Grit! you've got that, boy, a-plenty. But I said, 'trouble—deep trouble'. A feller has to have something to hang onto, something to want to live for to pull him through when real

3

trouble strikes. Do you love something or someone above all else that you would fight to live for?" My muscles tensed. "Yes sir, I do, It's the old farm homestead and the promise to my father on his deathbed that I would take it over and care for it and cherish this heritage of our forebears with honor. My father was a good and faithful man; my mother a saintly woman. Mother needs me now to care for the old home and make her latter days secure." The old man rose and went to his desk. "Well lad, I believe you've got what it takes to struggle out through that wilderness of cold and come back alive. I'll chance you on it!" And he handed me what I needed for outfit and fare to join my brother and hope to find even a little 'pot of gold'—just enough to pay off the debt on the old homestead was all I cared.

A.E. Ball Farm Home photographed about 1890

4

The following are some of my adventures, rugged indeed, which proved true these lines of the poet, Robert W. Service, who was one of the bright poets of the land of the midnight sun.

"This is the law of the Yukon, and ever she makes it plain:
Send not your foolish or feeble, Send me your strong and sane.
Them will I gild with my treasure; Them will I glut with my meat;
But the others,—the misfits and failures,—I trample under my feet."

View of Farm Buildings, A.E. Ball Farm

Grotesque Totem Poles Carved by the Alaska Indians

CHAPTER 2

Travelogue North

My cousins, Ethel and Charley Taylor, had moved onto the old home place to care for it while I was away, so my mind was at ease about my affairs. I took leave of all my neighbors and friends and started for the Klondike on August 6, 1900. My fare was $58 to Seattle, Washington, where I arrived on Aug. 11 and visited all my brothers, sister, and my mother in that area. As Seattle was the best place to buy supplies for the rigorous climate of the north, I laid in the following outfit:

6 pair wool socks	$ 3.00
2 pair German wool socks	2.00
2 pair mitts	3.00
2 wool blankets—8 lb.	12.00
2 pair hip boots	14.00
1 tarpaulin	4.50
1 cap	4.00
1 wool blanket—16 lb.	10.00
	$52.50

The Canadian Government did not allow anyone to come to that Klondike territory without bringing 500 lbs. of provisions along. There had been starving with shortage of food in Dawson, as no supply ships could get through after the Yukon river had frozen. This made it very hard because men had to pack everything on their backs over the mountain about 120 miles. There was a competition over ship fares at this time, so my ticket from Seattle to Dawson was only $68.

After bidding my mother and family all farewell, I took ship on *Queen of Alaska*, which was 320 feet long, and started our voyage on Aug. 23. It took five days to sail 1000 miles from Seattle to Skagway, Alaska, where we were to take a train. We sailed near the mainland, passed Vancouver Island, through Queen Charlotte's Sound where we were well rocked in 'the cradle of the deep', then passed through Dixon's Entrance and The Thousand Islands, all of volcanic origin. At this point a lighthouse marks the boundary line of our Alaskan territory. These islands have fir timber of good size and a great value to the United States. In the distance the mainland mountains were all capped with snow. At Ketchikan on Revillagigedo Island was the first town mostly inhabited by Indians, with totem poles of many kinds near the ocean shore. We made a stop of about one hour and were allowed to go ashore some 40 minutes. Walking among those totem poles seemed to make a person feel strange, as they were so large and all looking out over the ocean; one felt as though he was beneath their dignity to be noticed.

The first town of our Alaskan possessions was Wrangel, of 500 or 600 inhabitants. (in 1900). Here, standing out in bold relief upon the shore and 200 feet from tidewater, we observed many grotesque totem poles carved by the Alaskan Indians, and as before, the totem poles looked far out over the broad expanse of the great Pacific. They represented two distinct tribes, one having for its chief emblem the Eagle; the other the Raven; each tribe having its chief emblem carved on the top of the pole. When the son of a chief attained a certain age, the first animal he saw, be it a bear, frog, or any other animal, determined the lineal figure to be carved on his pole. A large totem pole was stolen from here and placed in a square in Seattle, but the city had to pay the Indians $10,000 for it.

Having taken in the sights here, we resumed our voyage amid islands and numerous icebergs and several spouting whales plowing the briny deep. At various points buoys marked out danger. There were also a number of houses at different points, and two small towns of minor importance were passed when the great Muir Glacier 200 feet high came into view on the mainland. It stretched 20 miles or more along the coast and as many back on the other side. Up on the mountain the springs freeze or run down its sides forming these glaciers, building out over the ocean till the great mass becomes so heavy, it breaks off, then becomes a floating iceberg. Only about one eighth of their bulk can be seen above the water's surface. These, with the dense fog, are very dangerous to navigation.

Passing through the Millbank Sound and westward about 100 miles, we arrived at Sitka, the Metropolis (in 1900) of Alaska, and which is on Baranof Island. The tide here rises some 22 feet, with rainfall from seven to 12½ feet each year and is 100 miles or so from the mainland on what is known as the Isthmain Canal. Sitka was founded by the Russians who built here a Russian Greek Catholic church. It is noted for its wealth and is perhaps 60 × 80 feet with an octagonal dome which let in the light from all sides. Several bells, each a different tone, beautifully chimed the hour of worship. Each sightseer paid 25¢. There was not a seat in the entire edifice but round the walls were many images shrined in beaten gold.

After two hours sightseeing in Sitka we hastened to our ship which followed what is called the Inland Channel. There were many islands and great icebergs among which our ship was constantly evading, making a very meandering course. The great Mural Glacier was at our right. There were several Russian forts still standing, and many totem poles such as at Wrangel. The natural scenery was superb and the United States Government was planning for a great park here. After leaving Sitka we rounded the island and passed through Rodman's Channel about eight miles wide. Several quartz mines were in sight at this point. The salmon were 'on the run' passing through the channel. They were jumping out of the water five or six feet and appeared as numerous as stalks of corn in our cornfields, so much so that, to look each way from our vessel the water was almost hid from view. Farther on there were several fish traps where the fish were lifted by an elevator and carried into the canneries. Indians did the canning, overseen by white men.

The next place of importance was Juneau. Near here the greatest quartz mines and stamp mills in the world are located, whose annual output of gold for the last two or three years was over $2,000,000. This mine alone will be worth more to the United States than the purchase price of Alaska, to say nothing of the vast forests and fisheries, besides other mineral wealth. Our next town was Dyea where there is a very deep quartz mine. The largest quartz mine in Alaska was said to be 3,000 feet deep.

Our last stop was at Skagway on the Lynn Canal Inlet of the Pacific Ocean. This was the gateway of the Klondike, yet 500 or more miles beyond. Skagway lies on a level plot of ground between abrupt mountains. It had (in 1900) 1000 inhabitants, and was the beginning of the White Pass and Yukon Railroad route. The town had many Indian curios; many were beaten from copper from native nuggets. Skagway is 126 miles to Whitehorse by rail and only 26 miles to the Canadian line.

Our ship came into port and in a short time the tide was out and we were sitting as it were on dry land. High tide at Skagway was usually 36 feet. We were told to stay aboard that night till the train would come next day and take us some 12 miles farther up in the mountains. While waiting there that evening I saw some of the men put on their new hip boots, go down to the beach and walk in the mud. Then they came on board ship, changed their boots to another pair and went down to the beach and repeated the performance, all of which seemed so strange to me.

The salmon were 'on the run'

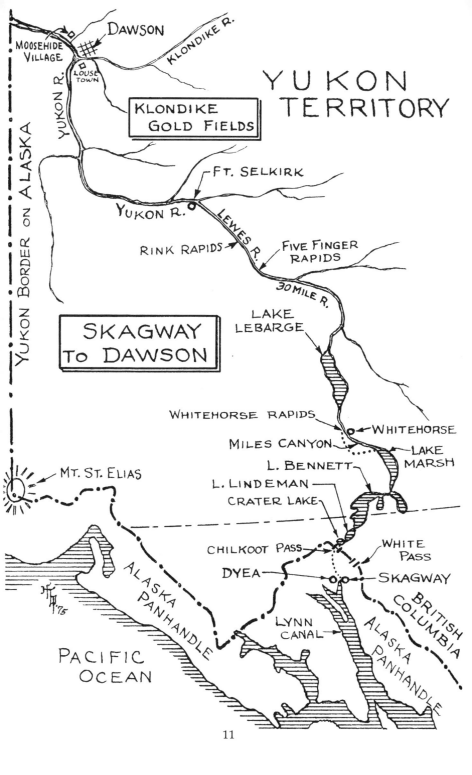

* * * * Chapter 3 * * * *

Up Chilkoot ~ Theodore Mercer

The next morning the train came, which was an engine and some flat cars. Each man had to load his outfit on, with the fare at 12 cents a mile and one dollar for each 100 lbs. for our baggage. We thought at the time this was extortion, but we soon found that $7.50 was very cheap when we unloaded our outfits and commenced to pack them over 100 miles. In climbing the mountains, two engines were used to pull the cars; the labor and slow progress of the engines proclaimed the grade of this wonderful road. Only the year before on July 6, 1899, this first railroad had been completed, starting at Skagway, skirting the mountains and lakes and ending at Whitehorse. When it was finished it offered a very great relief to the Klondikers, who before had to climb the almost vertical Chilkoot Pass trail with their packs to get over the mountains and into the Canadian territory. But this was not for us to ride in comfort by rail. We found that after its 12 mile run from Skagway, the railroad had to be temporairly closed to relocate some bridges and shorten its route. So this is where we had to leave the railroad and start packing our loads up the Chilkoot trail, which rose at 30° to 45° slope and entered Canada at the summit some 3500' above sea level.

We toiled up this mountain three long days to gain 10 miles, relaying our heavy packs as much as five times to reach the top. Because we had to relay our packs, this meant about 30 miles of actual hiking each day, and 15 miles of that we had to carry 120 lbs. Oh boy! How we did toil and camp on the trail! As it was still August, we trudged and plodded wearily to right or left, but always up the rugged ascent, wherever we could get a foothold. In winter it was more difficult, but steps had been cut into this icy way to make easier climbing, and a cable was fastened beside the trail for support. Occasionally one step was made wider so the weary one could step out of line to rest, but this often delayed him trying to get back into line again, and so on to the summit. To go back down for the next pack, the Klondiker just clambered down, or in winter, slid down a snow trail near the line of steps to the bottom, there to start all over again.

Here a few got to know one another. At night about 20 of us formed into a band or camp, wherever we stopped on the trail.

Before we passed timber line we had to gather enough wood and take it along to make a fire to burn all night, because the mountains were full of large timber wolves. Often someone in our band would shoot one of the wolves and the whole pack would devour it.

At the summit the Northwest Mounted Police were patroling the area, with customs officials to tax duty on all our new outfits, such as my store fresh hip boots. Here I had to pay $7 duty on each pair which was as much as they had cost me in Seattle. For my outfit, I paid $56 duty. *My* boots were *not soiled!* Now I knew why the men had waded in the mud! Oh boy! What it is to be a 'tenderfoot' or a 'greenhorn'!! Here all our packs were numbered and our names put on each pack of 120 lbs.; then we all had to be vaccinated or go back. This I evaded so as not to have a sore arm, as I was opposed to vaccination, and here was no alternative. By strategy and quietly on my part I determined without even a show of opposition, to let them vaccinate me. I went in and as I saw the procedure of what was required, I immediately took off my coat and bared my arm. The doctor, La Chapelle, used the serum needle about three times on the arm then ordered me to go to the stove and dry it in. Instead, I immediately pressed out the vaccine, put on my coat and went to the woods nearby. Here I sucked out the poison stuff until the blood ran quite freely, then returned to my burdens on the summit.

At Chilkoot Pass the Northwest Mounted Police screened all who came and so eliminated any known to be thugs or sharks such as 'Soapy' Smith and his gang who were 'con' men and tried to get Klondikers' cash both going and coming back. They also would not permit firearms or hand guns and so prevented much trouble in the rough mine camps. When we looked off to the left we could see the volcano Mount St. Elias 100 or 200 miles away. All the mountains were capped with ice and snow as far as the eye could see.

There were two men who died on the trail. One was Mike Mercer, a man with his brother who was packing near me. He was overheated and the vaccination seemed to poison his whole arm and side. This was about a week after he was vaccinated and made him suffer an awful painful death. His brother Theodore who was with him was so stricken with grief that he would moan and repeat over and over, "Returné, Returné! Mike! Mon cher Mike!" I tried to ease Theodore's load by buying some of Mike's outfit. "It's too much for you to carry, Theodore. Let me help you now." We burned the frozen ground and dug a grave about three feet deep. With small round poles we built his coffin and lined it with moss, then rolled him in his blankets, placed him in and laid the top over with short sticks. Then we covered all with moss and placed the ground over his grave. I never saw a brother weep as Theodore did, and he wanted to turn back. He was a Frenchman and talked so broken, I could scarcely understand. "Don't weep, Theodore," I pleaded, "I'll be a brother to you the best I can." He looked at me so strange through his tears as I took his hand to comfort him. "I'll always be your friend." This seemed to console him. He would nod his head as to give ascent, and though he could scarcely say anything in English he seemed to realize I was his friend, so we stayed together.

At the summit the Northwest Mounted Police were patroling the area

Chapter 4

Back Pack to Whitehorse

We finally got our packs all over the Chilkoot and down the northern slope which ended near Crater Lake. Here streams had filled up an extinct volcano and made this lake bottomless. As this was still August and warm after we got over the Chilkoot and I was always intrigued by daring to do the unusual, I had a swim in the icy waters of this lake and got refreshed. At this point a series of lakes, rivers, canyons and rapids rush, first calm then wild, in a headlong torrent forming the headwaters of the Yukon. Here many stout hearts, over Chilkoot, quailed at sight of the dangerous waters ahead and turned back home. Others, more foolhardy than wise, had slashed the trees from the hillsides, whipsawed them into rough lumber, and with unskilled hands had built makeshift rafts and boats, unsafe for such wild water. Thousands had capsized with their outfits; so the Northwest Mounted Police made a law. No one would be permitted to make boats or navigate them unless they were safe and their pilots skilled.

As we each had 600 lbs. of outfit, Theodore and I left most of our goods in a warehouse with duty and freight paid to Whitehorse when the railroad should reopen. Having still so many pounds of outfit to pack, we encountered the first real hardship of our journey, for it was 100 miles farther we must pack to Whitehorse. I was thankful that if I ever returned, the railroad would be completed from Whitehorse to Skagway and no need to pack. As it was, we packed overland but, those who could rafted down Lakes Lindemann, Bennett, Tagish and Marsh Lake; then the whirlpool and furious current of Miles Canyon, where the water is so compressed through the narrowed walls of solid basalt that it humps up several feet higher in the center, then shoots out in a torrent at the end leading to Squaw Rapids. Whitehorse Rapids are so dashed on the rocky stream bed that the water is lashed into a fury of white spume, like the flashing manes of white stallions galloping free.

Here at Whitehorse at last, we ended our hard pack on the overland journey from Chilkoot. We took the river steamer *Col* the last 400 miles down the waterways to the Yukon River, and so to Dawson. We passed through the Rapids, Lake Le Barge and

Thirty Mile River to the Five Finger Rapids. Here the rapids are formed by four great boulders, most resembling the abutments of a bridge, with five fingers of water rushing through between. Our boat was let through these rapids by a steel cable, wound or unwound on a winch by the boat's engines. After the Rink Rapids and the Lewes River, we sailed down the Yukon. Great mountains on either side of the Yukon were covered with moss and verdure most beautiful to behold, while here and there many wild sheep and goats were seen grazing on the slopes. At other points were moose, caribou, and bear; and at one place, coal mines, with coal at 10¢ a pound.

All newcomers to the Klondike were called 'Cheechako' or 'Tenderfoot'; but an oldtimer who had been mining for a year or so was known as a real 'Sourdough'. This latter term I found out was because miners kept a little can of sour dough (or fermented dough) by the warm stove in their cabins as a 'starter' or yeast for making pancakes and biscuits. So a 'Tenderfoot' I was, and destined to eat sourdough cakes until I had learned the ways of the North as a real pioneer.

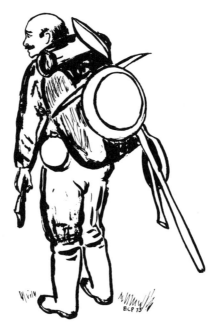

We each had 600 lbs. of outfit, and were called 'Cheechako' or 'Tenderfoot'

16

* * * * CHAPTER 5 * * * *

Dawson ~ Kinsley's Jobs ~ Theodore Again

On Sunday September 2, 1900, we landed safely at Dawson City and the first thing was to pay duty on my outfit which was bonded through. On several pairs of rubber boots and shoes I paid 33% on the dollar of investment, so I had only fifty two dollars left after all was paid. Here I bid farewell to Theodore Mercer and lost sight of him in a few days; but we remained good friends as long as I was in the Klondike. He was always asking my advice and many times came to see me, and was so attached, he wept when three years later I started to the outside and home.

About an hour after we docked, brother Kinsley got in from the claim where he worked and hailed me, "Halloo! 'Tenderfoot'! Sure good to see you!" "And you too!" I agreed, "I need a friend! Do you know they just about stripped my pockets with all that duty! I need a job right off!" "And that's just what I came to tell you. Construction work here is booming. They can't get enough men handy with a hammer and a know how about building. I got a lot of jobs lined up for you to start on right away. The new Klondiker Hotel is building and needs a carpenter this very hour." So that first afternoon in Dawson I earned six dollars and each day added my earnings at one dollar an hour. That was 16 times the wages of a farm worker back home.

I worked early and late for three weeks and averaged $15 a day, which was at that time of year mostly by candle light, because by Oct. 1 in the far north there was only a few hours daylight. I soon had $200 in gold dust as this was used for money there. Most of September I worked at carpentering; one was on a new store for G. Gibs, and many odd jobs. In October, having obtained a rifle, I hunted and got 14 rabbits and 10 grouse for which I was paid $20, but I nearly froze and was blind with frost. On October 5 I went to Quartz Creek and worked for Spech for $40. Then Kinsley, and his wife who had come along, were going to take work at the famous Lippy Claim on #16 Eldorado Creek and wanted me to go with them. I wanted to get a knowledge of placer mining here, but Lippy had no place open then.

On October 12 I went to see Crockett and look for work. Crockett was manager of the claim at #18 Below on Bonanza Creek, when I heard he wanted a man. I went at once on October

17

26 and got the job on this Crockett claim for $5 a day, or $120 a month, and board with cabin room. Mr. Crockett took me to the cabin and showed me my bunk which I fixed and rolled in. Next morning to my great surprise, there was Theodore Mercer, my 'adopted' brother. "Ball! Ball!" he cried as he came to me and gave his hand with smiles; and soon in tears was overjoyed to be with me again. He was my windlass man all that winter.

There were some of the men who tried to be smart and did some tricks on Mr. Mercer. They called him a 'Jap' and a 'Chinaman' because of his broken speech. This was so irritating to me that I admonished them severely. Then they turned on *me* with their derision and it got to be most unbearable. One day I was sitting on a chair, leaning forward mending a mitten when one named Bill Peterson came to my chair and straddled it between me and the back of the chair. Putting his hands on my bald head, he plagued, "My, oh my! Mr. Ball, what a bald head you have!" Quick as a cat I reached down and caught him under his knees and raised up with him on my back. I took a step or two, then let him fall on a pile of wood on the cabin floor, and I came down on top so hard, it knocked the breath out of him. I turned and grabbed his neck and drew my fist and said, "I could smash you in a minute, but will let you go this time if you will behave yourself!" He was so hurt he could hardly get his breath, and never again did he ever molest me or my 'adopted' brother.

Theodore was a French Catholic and a good man and we worked together all winter. The discomforts of that winter, 40° to 60° below zero, made me suffer with rheumatism so that I had to nail strips on the ridge pole above my bunk to enable me to rise each morning. Several times I worked 24 hours without sleep. Many miners died that winter of scurvy and spinal meningitis. I had worked for Crockett Nov. 1, 1900 through April 27, 1901 and received in 'dust', at $18 an oz., $604.70.

On several pairs of rubber boots and shoes I paid 33% on the dollar of investment

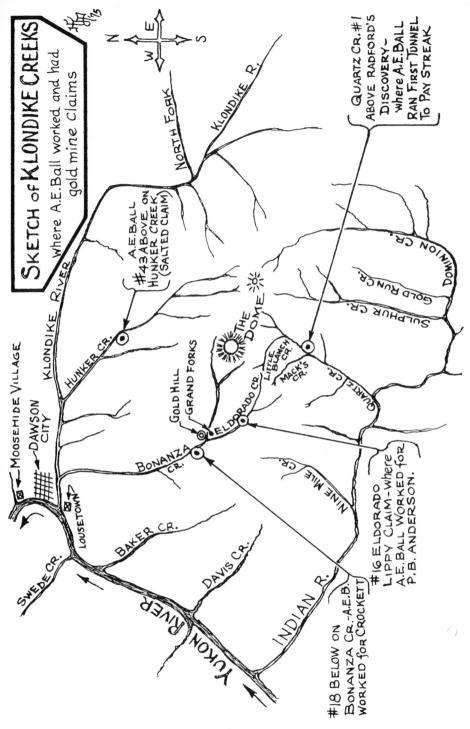

SKETCH of KLONDIKE CREEKS
where A.E.Ball worked and had
gold mine Claims

N E W S

MOOSEHIDE VILLAGE
DAWSON CITY
LOUSETOWN
SWEDE CR.
YUKON RIVER
KLONDIKE RIVER
HUNKER CR.
NORTH FORK
KLONDIKE R.

A.E.BALL
#43 ABOVE on
HUNKER CREEK
(SALTED CLAIM)

QUARTZ CR. #1
ABOVE RADFORD'S
DISCOVERY —
where A.E.BALL
RAN FIRST TUNNEL
To PAY STREAK

THE DOME

LITTLE
BLANCH
CR.
MACK'S
CR.
DOMINION CR.
GOLD RUN CR.
SULPHUR CR.
QUARTZ CR.

GOLD HILL
GRAND FORKS
ELDORADO CR.
BONANZA CR.
NINE MILE CR.

BAKER CR.
DAVIS CR.
INDIAN R.

#18 BELOW on
BONANZA CR. — A.E.B.
WORKED for CROCKETT

#16 ELDORADO
LIPPY CLAIM — where
A.E.BALL WORKED FOR
P.B. ANDERSON.

19

Chapter 6

Lippy Claim ~ Widow Purdy ~ P.B. Anderson

I was now going on April 28 to where my brother worked at #16 Eldorado Creek, as I now found work on this Tom Lippy Claim. The rivers freeze over solid from October through May, so no boats can get through then. But by April 27 there had been a rain and thaw and that made quite a flood. I took my leave of all the boys at Crockett's, especially my 'brother', Theodore Mercer, and started with all my belongings. When I had gone about two miles, I came to where the high water bridge across Bonanza Creek was washed away. It was perhaps 60 feet across the water, and looked to be two feet deep and quite swift. I sized it up and decided to wade across; so unpacked my travelling bag and got out my hip boots. I took off my shoes, exchanged them for my hip boots and waded across all right.

I was just about to change again when I saw a woman coming. When she got to the other side I called to her, "What will you do now?" "I don't know what to do", she replied, "I'm in a desperate situation!" "Well, I got across all right. If you are willing to risk it, maybe I could carry you across. How much do you weigh?" "165 pounds. That's a lot for you." "Well, I packed over Chilkoot, so I've had practice. I believe I can do it." "Good! I'll chance it!" So I started across for her. I got her 'grip', which was quite a heavy one, and took that across first, then returned for her. I had her walk up on a log that lay across another log thrown up on the bank by the force of the water. She was then about two feet above the ground and in a good position for me to take her on my back.

I reached around her knees and told her to put her arms around my shoulders and be careful not to choke me and to sit very still. I started down to the water's edge and said "Giddap! horsey!" and carried her across safely. In the deepest water I could barely keep her feet out of the torrent, but my feet were firmer set with the added weight. When I put her down, "Yes", she agreed, "you made a good horsie, and I do thank you." We had a good laugh and continued on to her claim on Gold Hill, where she asked me to eat dinner with them. She had been to Dawson to see a lawyer about one of her claims, of which a man was trying to claim ownership. She had four men working for her and was making good. She had been left with her four children when her husband, Mr. Purdy, had died suddenly with pneumonia. When I had enjoyed her good dinner and was starting, she would not let me go until I had accepted one dollar for carrying her across the creek.

I later learned that the Dawson lawyer, George Black, was settling Mrs. Purdy's late husband's estate, and this began their friendship. He was the Attorney Black who was elected by the miners to represent Yukon Territory in the Canadian Parliament and became Governor of the Yukon. Mrs. Purdy and George Black were married in 1904. Later he became Speaker of the House, and in 1935 when her husband was ill, Mrs. Black was elected to the House of Commons at Ottawa. They resided many years at Whitehorse, where she was affectionately known as 'The Grand Old Lady of the Yukon'.

Leaving Mrs. Purdy at Gold Hill and again on my way, I came to my brother's place at the famous Lippy Claim, #16 Eldorado Creek, where $2,000,000 was taken out. Working about two weeks, April 28 through May 11, I helped wash up $650,000 of gold dust there, and on May 23 received $165 (10 oz. 6p. 7g. in gold dust) from J. D. Putrun, in full for this account of work. On this Thomas Lippy claim was where I worked for P. B. Anderson. I helped him build two cabins, flume and sluice boxes, and rockers for washing out gold, and also made tables and chairs. Mr. Anderson had his wife and three young children there with him. I well remember their little girl, who, when grown, became Ethel Anderson Becker, author of 'Klondike '98', depicting many of the Hegg photographs.

While working at Lippy's claim, my brother's wife had a baby boy, born dead. "I will make a little coffin and bury him for you", I told the grieving parents. Mr. Lippy gave me some boards and said, "Take these and anything else you need and use my shop to build it." So I made a tiny coffin and lined it with some cloth that the mother had and placed the child in it. With great sorrow they took leave of their little son. I went a half mile up into the mountains where, between two huge rocks 16 inches apart, I dug the small grave, placed the tiny coffin in it and carefully covered it. I then put stones over the top so that wolves or dogs could not molest the little tomb; then with my pick cut 'A.B.' on the side of the great rock. This was one of the saddest trials of my life; but knowing that nature and nature's God was the only hope, I returned to their cabin and consoled the sorrowing parents, assuring them their little son was safe; and they felt it was the best that could be done in that far away land of ice and snow.

I started down to the water's edge and said "Giddap! horsey!" and carried her across safely

* * * * CHAPTER 7 * * * *

#43 Hunker Creek ~ Up King's Dome

During May 12 through 29 I had worked at #14 and #15 Eldorado Creek and was paid by James Couse for this work $153.60 gold dust. I soon was getting larger wages repairing flumes and sluice boxes and rockers. By the first of May 1901 I had saved $1500, and near this time I heard of a claim a man had for sale as he was about to leave for the outside. I was still a 'Tenderfoot' for I had not been in the country one year; yet I had learned to pan and in a general way, to run a mine. On June 10 I bought the half interest in this claim at #43 above Discovery on Hunker Creek. I bought from a man by the name of Fred Zahn who said the claim was good, and paid him $500 in gold dust for a tent and tools and food supplies.

It was June 10 after buying the interest in this claim, that I purchased some mining tools at Grand Forks, Bonanza Creek, thinking it might be my last chance to procure them. With these tools and a good supply of blankets, I started up the trail on the mountainside to the new government road leading to the noted Dome Roadhouse. This was on the mountain back of Dawson. These roadhouses were started here and there over the creeks, not only to feed and rest the weary miners as they travelled hiking from creek to creek, but also to be storehouses of provisions from which to supply their needs without going all the way to Dawson. They also had accomodations as centers of recreation to relieve the drudgery and monotony, even the boredom of a miner's life. At times they had meetings and celebrations at the roadhouses such as one celebrating the Queen's birthday, with a photograph of this assemblage which I have, that was taken by the light of the midnight sun. Here I got my evening meal and took quite a good rest, as I had already gone 35 miles and had four miles more to go to reach my claim.

When I was ready to start, I placed my load upon a bench where I could more easily adjust my pack strap on my back, and again started. The government road at this place veered off to the right, and again I had to take the foot trail along the King's Dome for a mile to where the trail veered down to the left. Here at this point, I placed my load on a rock, and proceeded with one blanket to climb to the topmost part of the Dome, or possibly 200 feet higher up which I thought I might reach about midnight, and I did. Here I was 4000 feet above sea level, and Oh Boy! was I tired! This most lofty height gained, I procured a seat on a rock with my back against another rock, and wrapped in my blanket I surveyed the country around.

This being the tenth day of June, I judged that by the sixteenth or eighteenth of June the sun would be far enough to the north to shine past the north pole of the earth. It was already causing the stars and moon to dim by making a strong twilight such as we never see or know back here in the states. Again I returned down to where I had left my burden, and sure it was there as I had left it. I took up my pack, carefully adjusted my pack straps, and down, down that narrow trail till I was nearly to the timber line.

Here I found a broken castaway hand sled that suggested to me that I might relieve myself of my heavy weighing burden; as it was much harder to carry a heavy load down a steep trail than to carry the same load up. Again I unloaded and rested a few minutes, then drew out the draw cord of my 'war bag'. By tearing into strips two large handkerchieves, I succeeded in binding the broken runner of the sled. Now I could drag my load down the mountainside, which was a great relief, as I could now by my weight quite easily draw the sled on the bare ground at such a steep descent. Several times I sat down and rested and my courage began to come back. It seemed to remind me of a song I used to sing when less than one year before, we were climbing the Chilkoot Pass. The song was something like this:

"I met a wayworn traveller in tattered garments clad,
His back was heavy laden, it seemed that he was sad;
But he kept pressing onward, for he was wending home.
So then do your best for one another, making life a pleasant dream,
Help a worn and weary brother, pulling hard against the stream."

And with such thoughts in mind, I arrived at my journey's end about nine o'clock the eleventh of June. When Mr. Marinan, my partner, saw me drag in, he was concerned. "Here, you lie down on my bunk and rest, while I get you something to eat. You look tuckered!" "Well, I've had nothing to eat since six o'clock yesterday. Guess I'll appreciate some food, and thank you. I'll turn in for awhile." I slept about two hours, then ate and slept again.

CHAPTER 8

Bear ~ Seeing Earth Turn ~ Claim 'Salted'

Mr. Marinan and I worked with a good will. I told him about my interest in astronomy and of my first hike to the King's Dome. "Marinan, I have it all figured out! If I can go again to the King's Dome on the 17th of June and observe for about two days, within that time the sun should be rising over the North Pole and the Rocky Mountains, and I surely would like to see this phenomenon." "That will work out fine," Marinan agreed, "We'll need more provisions by then. I'd rather stay here and work on the claim anyway, if that's all right with you." It sure was! So again I started for the King's Dome at three o'clock, with my pack strap and a very light sled on my back and a good cudgel in each hand, up and up 3000 feet. I had left my gun at the cabin to have less weight to carry, and had only my jack knife along.

When about half way I thought I heard something above me. On looking up, to my horror, there stood up in the trail a large bear only 20 feet before me. Dumfounded, I stood still and eyed the huge beast, and he seemed to be eyeing me also. My heart thumped so hard I could hear it pound. Seconds seemed as minutes; but presently he got down on all fours and began to move away; then up on hind legs and eyed me sharply. I continued to stand until he finally scuttled off through the brush and I thought he was a good safe distance away. Then I recalled that I had complied with the standing Ad in the *Dawson Daily News*, —to stand still if you should meet a bear on the trail, which I had unconsciously done.

Proceeding on my way, I arrived at the summit of the Dome at half past eleven and ate my lunch. The twilight had put the moon and stars to sleep for the short Arctic summer. I took the same position I had seven days before, and in the northeast the sun was rising and showed about one half of its diameter for some 20 minutes, then sank out of sight, but it was as bright as day. I went to the Roadhouse and stayed all night, or till eleven the next night. During the day I had bought my supplies of provisions at Cook's Roadhouse, which included these items: 100 lb. spuds—$32.00; 25 lb. bacon—$7.00; ½ gal. can honey—$2.40; 3 lb. dried apples—$1.20; 50 lb. flour—$15.00–$18.00; 1 doz. eggs—$2.00.

Arriving again on the King's Dome, I saw that the sun was fast ascending. The Rocky Mountains, which are just west of the McKenzie River, were plainly visible and perhaps 80 or 90 miles away. Seeing the earth turn, I could only stand dumb to the wondrous thrill I received. In the month of June, just a few days before the sun was clear above the tops of the mountains, far away to the north, the revolution of the earth to the east brought the mountains between me and the sun, where I was on the King's Dome. The sunbeams seemed to be and really were passing between me and the mountains.

The mountains were rushing past the face of the sun at the rate of about 470 miles an hour. The sight was wonderful, to see the earth turning at such a terrific speed; and the sun beyond those snow capped icebound mountains, with the great searchlight shadows all colors of the rainbow, and these colors changing in such rapid succession. It declared the glory of an eternal Creator, and God whose work and power is far past finding out. But perfect in their ample rounds, no one deviating from the path prescribed by the hand of their all wise Creator, the one hundreth part of a minute in a thousand years. I was awed by the great phenomena before me, and had a sense of fear lest I might forget and make a fatal step to the side and plunge to the rocky depths below. This scene lasted for the space of 30 minutes.

You may wonder why I say at the speed of 470 miles an hour, which is approximately correct, as the distance from the Arctic Circle is, or where the phenomena occurred is, about 24° south of the North Pole. Counting each degree as 68½ miles, the distance from the Arctic Circle to the North Pole would be 1,644 miles. Twice that distance would be the diameter of the circle, or 3,288 miles, the circumference would be 11,273 miles, and this divided by 24 hours would be 470 miles an hour. If I would have had my compass there, I could have procured the correct distance to the mountains where the phenomena occurred. The diurnal motion of the earth very plainly shows the turning of the earth.

Returning with all this grand vision of the heavens, I tried to tell my partner what it was like, but he was strangely quiet. "Mr. Ball, I believe I've discovered something too, only of more concern to us than the earth's turning in the sky." My interest plummeted at once from the heavens to the earth beneath my feet. "You know that Zahn who sold us this claim, and how he scraped around a bit and came up with a little gold dust in the pan! I believe he was a scoundrel and 'salted' it! I went all over that place, and not a bit more gold was there!" "Are you sure?" I cried. "Don't tell me I've lost again! Maybe we should test a wider area more carefully!" And so we did until September 8, when the total from July 10 cleaned up only $165.35. We also heard that Zahn had left for California, and had gone down the Yukon to Nome, Alaska. From Nome he had taken passage on *The Islander,* which struck an iceberg and sank in 3000 feet of water near Dyea. All on board were saved, but the $2,000,000 in gold was in the purser's office and was lost. Zahn's deception did not benefit him for long.

Mr. Marinan had been a good partner and was a great man to work, so as he already owned the other half of the claim at #43 above on Hunker Creek, I sold him my interest and bade him goodbye. Disgusted, I took my outfit and left for my brother's new place on Quartz Creek. Feeling much depressed, I promised myself to work only for wages the rest of the time in this bleak and forbidding country, which had such promise, then snatched it from my hand.

Don't tell me I've lost again! Maybe we should test a wider area more carefully!

CHAPTER 9

Kinsley and A. E. at Quartz Creek—Frozen Blind

At Quartz Creek my brother Kinsley, with Wilson and Roper, had a claim in partnership which they were getting ready to work. Brother and wife had a little store there. They also had a garden in the delightful sunny, but short, summer just past. Temperatures varied from 90° in summer to 50° to 85° below zero in winter. On Sept. 12, 1901 I started work for Brother cutting wood, and built a small cabin for him at $5 a day and board. I also did a number of other odd jobs, hoping a chance for me might turn up. I had scarcely finished the cabin when Brother and company wanted 300 cords of wood cut, so I got this job at $3 a cord, then hauled it to fire their boilers. The boilers made steam to thaw the deeply frozen 'permafrost.' The steam under pressure went through pipes and a crosshead with steel points which were driven into the frozen earth to thaw it. The earth was then loosened with a pick, and was dug out from the pay streak, later to be washed up to get the gold.

And so with the wood hauling job came the need for a horse, and I set out to find one. It was mid October and getting very cold, especially on the mountain trails. Horses were hard to find, let alone one for sale, but I had heard of one and was on my way home. I'd get the horse next day.

I was getting very tired, even sleepy. My footsteps were only inching ahead. I shook myself. "Stay awake! Keep going! You can make it,—you've got to!!" An inner voice urged me on. My legs plodded like lead. I could scarcely see or feel. The breeze stiffened on the high summit trail and I suddenly was shocked into the seriousness of my plight. I was warmly clothed, and in the valley where the air was dry and calm I would not have noticed it, but with that breeze and deadly cold at 72° to 84° below, for the second time this winter, I began to realize that I was nearly frozen. I must keep moving or perish. So I struggled desperately on a few more rods. Then,—oh what deliverance!— a cabin!! Thank God for the Northwest Mounted Police and their law of the Yukon. This excellent police staff required these shelter cabins on the trails to be always provided with kindling, matches and food for lone travellers in just such emergencies as I was in, and saved many lives from a tragic end. I was so blind and stiff I could scarcely strike a match, but did manage to build a fire on the cabin's ground floor. Then I held my tarpaulin around it to get heat till my sight gradually came back. It took several hours to get thoroughly warmed, and after such a close call, my thoughts began to take stock of my situation.

Here I was some 3,500 miles from home, way off here in the Klondike Gold Rush in the fall of 1901; and now my life had been all but lost, but for this timely refuge. So many discouragements had followed my efforts this past year. I was a 'Tenderfoot' and had to learn by sad experience. I had worked some 12 months for wages, then lost it all in that worthless mine; so all my money and my first year's labor was lost. But now, with this deliverance from the freezing cold, there surely was a God who cared and must have some great good ahead if I but renewed my courage, trust and hope. Warmed and grateful, I then faced the frigid breeze and plodded on another half mile or so to reach my brother's cabin.

That evening I got out my diary and reread my first hopeful entries of a year ago. On the flyleaf in bold print, my name, "AMOS ENTHEUS BALL, age 41, weight 146." I had always been small like my indomitable little mother, who at 15 had tamed and taught a log schoolfull of backwoods boys near 20. The Balls of my father's line were giants of men; but, despite my small stature, I had sinews of steel, tenaceous grit and strength of mind, and I held my own.

The first address in my diary my mother had written when I had bade her farewell: 'Eliza Jane Early Ball'. It was she who had searched out my name, 'Entheus' from her Greek dictionary. It meant a zealous individual; one having God within; inspired. She meant me to have a name to live by. My circuit riding grandfather, the Reverend Amos Ball, had given my first name. He had ridden horseback on the forest trails of western Pennsylvania with his saddlebags filled with the sacred Scriptures and the hymns of Charles and John Wesley, and with these had brought needed courage and comfort to the isolated settlers. I was pioneer bred and knew rugged life. I too could face these northern wilds. So, reliving my year with courage renewed, this was the entry I put in my diary that night: "It is not ease and facility that tends to bring out the good that is in a man, so much as trials and difficulties. Adversity is the touchstone of character. As some herbs need to be crushed to bring forth their sweetest odors, so some natures are tried by suffering to evoke the excellence that is in them."

This excellent police staff required these shelter cabins on the trails

* * * * CHAPTER 10 * * * *

Trains Horse ~ Hauls Wood

The next day I finally found and bought the only horse available. "He's the balkiest horse I ever did see," deplored the owner. "I never could do anything with him, and was about to sell him for dog meat. You can have him for $80, including his harness, and I'll give you that old broken sled to boot." That sounded fair enough, so I fixed the sled and got him hitched. We started, or tried to start with the sled, and then when he did start with all his might, I tried to hold him in. But no, he ran a mile, then off down a hill at the side of the road and lodged against a stump. I had to whip him; then for $2 got a man with his horse to haul the sled back on the road. I hitched him in my sled as best I could, but he still did not want to go.

At last I cut a strong stick three feet long; split a strap in two and made a good lash, and tried to start him again. He still refused, so I applied the lash around his flanks with all my strength. He became uneasy, then started with all his might. I let him go and held him in the road, and when he had gone more than a mile, he wanted to slacken up, but I would apply the lash with much vigor and did not let him stop till I saw he was very tired. Then I holloed 'Whoa!' and he stopped as nice as any horse. I let him rest a few minutes and then asked him to go, but as he hesitated, I showed him the whip, so he started again and trotted off awhile, then slowed down to a walk and I found that he was cured. I patted and praised him after that. "You were a good horse all the time. You just had to learn obedience, didn't you! Now we'll get along fine." "Never thought you could train that ornery beast," cried the surprised man, "I believe you've got a good worker now."

Next, the horse had to be shod and fed, so I got shoes on him for $12, also 125 lb. oats for $12 and 800 lb. of wild hay. On Oct. 14 I got these supplies in Dawson, also a good bobsled for $30 so we could haul the wood. Because of the intense cold I built a stable for my horse, and then made a suit of clothes out of gunny sacks for his legs. I always kept a double thickness of blankets on him under his harness, then dug and melted ice for him to drink, and also kept a nose bag on for him to breath in. The nose bag would collect with ice as his breath would freeze; so I would slip off the nose bag, knock the ice off and put it on again. He proved to be a very good horse. He had three nostril holes through which he breathed, and a large moustache, the largest I ever saw, which made him a curiosity. Hauling wood and freight in this way, I worked long hours for two months and earned a considerable sum, then sold the horse and sled with blankets for the price I paid.

Then I halloed 'Whoa!' and he stopped as nice as any horse

CHAPTER 11

Ancient Landslide ~ Buys Into #1 Above

While still hauling wood in December over that high summit trail, one day, I was suddenly stopped short in my tracks. An idea flashed into my mind! The whole mountainside with its valley spread out before me and reason took command. Just look, I thought, at this wonder of nature! These mountains and how they were formed! I stood in awe of the mightiness of it all. Then my eye caught an oddity never seen before—a dip on the side of the mountain, and a bulge. It looked as if at some ancient day a great landslide had scooped out that dip and tumbled its rocks and earth all over the stream bed at its base. This had shoved the stream way out a hundred feet or more, making a new course there, then curved its flow around the bulge to the normal course the original stream bed had. Gold is found along the bedrock of the stream, and for the length of two claims around that bulge, no gold had been found; but there were good finds of gold above and below the bulge. As the general range of mountains was straight, the old original channel must be straight, but the new channel around the bulge was quite crooked.

I conceived the idea that the pay streak was along the original stream bed 100 feet nearer the mountain. That explained why no gold had been found along this bulge, where they worked only along the present stream bed. This idea came to me as a vision, and nothing could gainsay it. I was determined to get that claim and try my hopes once more. That night at Brother's, I told him my idea, but he only laughed and remonstrated with me. "I thought you were smarter than that, Entheus! To sink money in a claim where men have found no gold and proved it's no good, is just plain foolishness." I had made over $600 hauling wood, and also freight from Dawson 32 miles away, so now I lost no time in going to see the men who had gone broke at this point on the creek.

In a few days I had a quit claim from the owners at #1 above Radford's Discovery on Quartz Creek. These men also laughed, "What a crazy idea!" they railed. "You must like to lose money!" They signed over all their rights and said it would not cost me anything. But I thanked them and gave them $5 gold dust, and asked if they would help me prospect it. "Not on your life!" they scoffed, "we've had enough of that claim!" "I could find that gold in a month's time," I promised, but no one was interested. Finally one fellow by the name of Hayden listened. He had been out of work for awhile and needed a job. "Well," he drawled, "it's a foolhardy job, but if you'll gaurantee me $5 a day and board, I guess I could help you that long." I had already figured I could run a tunnel back to the pay streak in just about a month's time so I accepted Bill Hayden's offer and began to gather up equipment to work the claim. I hired a boiler and thawing outfit for testing the ground and had an option on it if I wished to buy it, and so we commenced to work on Feb. 12, 1902.

I had already figured I could run a tunnel back to the pay streak in just about a month's time

* * * * CHAPTER 12 * * * *

Tunnel to Pay Streak ~ Wolves ~ Anderson and Scavdale Join

With great hopes ahead I bent my whole strength to the task of digging that tunnel. This is where my knowledge of surveying served me well. My father, Amos Walton Ball, had been surveyor of Jasper County, Illinois in the 1850's; and then at the old home in Western Pennsylvania there was often someone who needed land surveyed. Father taught me this skill, so I had helped him many times. I figured carefully the slopes and angle required, then started to tunnel at a decline of 20 feet to the 100 feet. This all was tediously slow rough work, and cold, as inch by inch the frozen earth was thawed and picked away, and the tunnel began to take shape underground. I had plenty of onlookers, as miners would come that way to gape at this new approach to a mine. As it was winter, it was dark all the time, and we had to work by candlelight, but my sure vision spurred me on.

At some 100 feet back into the mountainside, on the 29th day just as I had figured, I got a pan that washed up 5¢ of gold, which is considered good; then 9¢ and 20¢ to the pan! The pay streak had been struck! No more scoffing now! The news went along the creek. I was sure now my vision was true, and I immediately went and bought one half interest in the next claim below, with Mr. Scavdale on Radford's Discovery. At this time Bill Hayden wanted me to take him in as a partner, which I did for the term of the lease, providing he would promise me not to drink or gamble any more, until the lease ran out the next October, when we had to give up to the owners. I bought the boiler and thawing outfit, which was necessary to do good work. Bill Hayden had two dogs which were good help to drag wood down the hill. He hauled the wood while I cut down the trees and cut off the brush. This wood was to fire the boiler to make steam.

We needed another wheelbarrow, and I heard of one for sale seven miles away, so took my pack strap and went and bought it for $10 on March 14 and carried it on my back. I was coming on a very poor trail and the night came on before I got home. Then a pack of wolves began to howl and were coming so threateningly near that I was afraid. If the pack got to me there would be no escape. I had a hatchet in my hand to blaze some trees on the

35

Gardner's Road House ~ Quartz Creek, Yukon Territory ~ May 23, 1903, 10:30 P.M. Photograph taken by the light of the Midnight Sun

trail, which I could scarcely see for darkness. My heart was pounding as the wolves began to close in around me. Then with a sudden impulse I grabbed that hatchet and pounded hard, like shots on the wheelbarrow, and the wolves were frightened away, so I got back to my cabin safe and grateful.

At this time, the middle of March 1902, it was now near the daylight time; the snow began to melt and the water to flow in the creeks. We whipsawed some lumber planks to run our wheelbarrows on, and had some provisions in our mine in cold storage. By the 10th of May 1902, we had commenced thawing and bringing out the pay dirt and dumping it in our sluice boxes, when my partner, William Hayden, began to go down the creek to a roadhouse, where he began to drink. One day he came home and bragged, "Well, I made $20 today, gambling!" "Bill," I admonished him, "you promised you would not drink or gamble if I took you in as a partner." "Well," he countered, "I'll never go over $20." "Yes, but you will," I persisted, well knowing the temptation that lures addicts.

So in a few days he wanted to go down the creek again and was gone three days. One evening he came home so drunk, I had to help him in. He mumbled, "Lost it! Lost it! I've lost all my 'dust',"—which was near $1400. The fraction was nearly worked out and the pay was good, so that in about the three days Bill was gone, working alone, I took out $200. With this I took and paid the lease rent of over $300 and quit the fraction. Besides, I had to pay Bill's share in the boiler and tools. Then Bill wanted me to take him in on the claim I had bought a half interest in with Mr. Scavdale on Radford's Discovery. I would not do so, and he and his dogs left as poor as when they came.

Charley Anderson, a man I knew, then came and wanted to buy in with Mr. Scavdale and myself. He was known to be a good fellow, so we took him in as a partner. We cut a good supply of wood and snared 300 rabbits and put them in cold storage in boxes down in our mine which was always frozen. We then sawed some lumber and I made some sluice boxes. We built a new boiler house, then began to run a tunnel at the lowest end of our claim, which was 250 feet long. We were about a month running the tunnel and hauling our wood on the claim.

Chapter 13

Lose Trail ~ Camp With Indians ~ George Black

That summer of 1902 my partner, Charley Anderson, and I heard of some gold finds and went on a trip up the Klondike River stream to stake some claims. When we got there however, we found the ground had all been taken and staked. We crossed the mountain in order to strike a new trail for Dawson. At a point where the trail forked, we took the wrong way and soon heard noises and saw a light down in a small valley. In going on a little we found ourselves at the camping ground of the Moosehide Indians who were hunting there. We felt it was safer to camp with them than near them as darkness was coming on.

I had seen the chief at his camping place near Dawson and knew he was a great smoker, so I told Charley, "when we come into their camp give the chief some of your tobacco and that will please him and gain his favor." We saw some young Indian boys and asked, "Chief Isaacs—where is he?" They pointed in the direction of his tepee. Soon we were in Chief Isaac's commodious palace of moosehides. His tepee looked to be 18 feet in diameter, with moosehides to fit the large floor. In the center was an open spot laid around with stones for their fire which seemed quite cozy. So much of the smoke as did not find its way out of the hole in the top of the tepee, you got in your eyes. It was part of your hospitality.

We shook hands with the chief and explained that we were lost on our trail. Then Chief Isaacs rose up to his full stately height, and thumping his fists on his chest, exclaimed with great amusement, "What! You good Boston boys! You lost! Indian never get lost! Indian always right here!" Anderson got out his pipe and tobacco and offered some to the chief. "Have some. It's the best!" he smiled. Isaacs rolled some in his hand and sniffed, then filled his pipe. "Ah—great smoke!" and he seemed much pleased. I told the chief I had seen him at Dawson when he came home from his trip which the steamship company had given him to California. The chief talked with us in a broken way which we enjoyed, although a tired man would as leave handle the words whole as broken. It was not however 'Home, Sweet Home' among the aborigines, but 'in Rome do as the Romans do'; so we unrolled our blankets and were very careful to be well lapped in them. A. Ball rolls in nicely when it comes to getting abed.

The next morning Chief Isaacs insisted that we have breakfast with him, but when we saw the steaming kettle of roots, fish heads and tails with scales, plus rice which was supplied them by the Government, we were loath to accept this hospitality. However we were afraid of offending the chief so I nudged Charley. "We've got to make a pretense of eating some of that stew, along with our own sandwiches we have." Charley made a wry face, then swallowed hard, and I did the same. "Great soup, Chief; good and hot" we chirped. At least we managed to down some of it and survive.

After giving us directions to find the trail, we asked the Chief, "How far to Dawson?" He held up four fingers, "Four hours", which meant 12 miles. Chief Isaacs then shook hands with us and made me promise to come visit him at his village of Moosehide near Dawson. This I later did; and so we were on our way. When out of sight, we unrolled our blankets and carefully shook them for fear of lice. We were not over anxious to carry off any property of this kind Indian—not even a mite. The Moosehides are well provided with this kind of 'livestock', which can be readily taken by an attachment. We continued on our journey and by noon we were at Dawson.

About this time a man came to our area who was canvassing the creeks to get votes to be elected to the Canadian House of Commons. All who had a miner's license could vote, whether they were Canadian or of any other country. Mr. Scavdale's wife cooked several meals for him and he seemed to be a very good man. We went to two speeches he made on our creek and he was later elected by a good majority over his opponent. He was the Dawson lawyer, George Black, who later in 1904 married the Widow Purdy, whom I had carried over the swollen creek. Some time later he became Speaker of the House at Ottawa.

The camping ground of the Moosehide Indians

* * * * Chapter 14 * * * *

Terror in the Mine ~ Home News Sad ~ Charlie's Trick

On August 23, 1902 at 1:30 A.M., while working in our mine, I was nearly crushed by a large fall of frozen muck which scraped my shoulder, knocked the lantern out of my hand and mashed it flat, and so left me in total darkness. The terrific noise so badly frightened me that I became instantly nauseated with shock and could not stand. Had my end come? Had I been buried alive? I felt for the planks on the floor of the mine and crawled on my hands and knees in the darkness to where I could finally see out of the tunnel to the light. Then my trembling ceased and I felt great relief. I found my way to the boiler house where I improvised another lantern from a large tin can and a candle. Then, not knowing whether it was safe, I returned to the mine to clear out the muck and make ready for my partners and found all was right again. Evidently the steam had loosened the muck and about six or seven tons had fallen on our tunnel way. By a strange coincidence, it was at this very same time and hour that my brother Ellsworth was shot back home in Pennsylvania. His was one more tragedy caused by drinking alcohol and gambling.

That was the second sad news I had received from home since being in the Klondike. The first was the untimely death of a young neighbor man who was on construction work for the railroad. A heavy worn out chain broke and struck him as he worked nearby. The hazard had been reported but the company took no action to make it safe. This neighbor had one time worked for me on my farm. Ashtabula, Ohio was then building its fine harbor, so he helped me clear out the old stone fence rows on our farm and deliver the stone to the lake port. At news of his passing in 1901 I had written his widow to express my condolence, and she had replied. After a few months I had written again, and so began a friendly exchange of news.

Late in the summer of 1902 I had written her, but several months went by with no reply. My partner, Charley Anderson, noticed my disappointment when I found no mail, and slyly joked me about it. Then I thought it best to read again her last letter, which I did, and there I found instead of hers, my own last letter to her that had never been mailed. I couldn't understand

40

why I had been so careless as to so mix my letters, and at once sat down and wrote her the following:

"Quartz Creek, Oct. 23, 1902. Respected friend; I was somewhat surprised this evening in looking over my letter box to find a letter that I had written for you and thought it had been sent to you. I often write several letters at a time. I cannot find your letter to me, so it seems to me that probably I returned your letter through a mistake. If so, excuse me for doing so. I was very glad to hear from you and to know that you and the children are well and enjoying life. I have had sad news of my brother's death, which I could hardly think was true. My prayer is that he may meet his Maker with all things right. I am a poor hand to mourn as mourning does not better circumstances, but feel more determined to do what I think is right and look up for more light and truth to guide from error's ways. The bright side of life is the highway to success and happiness. Though I have had many trials and sorrows, yet the sunshine of a good hope has been sufficient to drive away the clouds of gloom and reveal new beauties never known except by trials taught. Trials often unmask virtues.

"Well, I must change off and tell you that I will be here one year more if all goes well, and then I will go back home. We have snow and the creeks are all frozen over. I have two good partners to work with. This winter we will take out pay dirt, as we call it, and wash it out in the spring. The ground is frozen here to a great depth and never thaws out. We have a boiler to thaw the ground. We have daylight from seven in the morning till five in the evening, but soon will have only five or six hours light. Will close with respects to you and family. A.E. Ball. Write and ask me anything you wish to know about this country and I will answer as best I can."

Note: This is to say how very nearly my hopes and dreams had *not* come true. The next year, just before my leaving for home, my partner Charley Anderson came to me in deep embarassment with conscience stricken words. "Ay tank I ask you forgive me, and hope all's vell vit your vidow. Ay meant no harm—youst a leedle yoke. Ay svitch your vidow's letter zat time." It was laughable then, but it could have nipped in the bud my only romance. So 'all's well that ends well', as the saying goes. Had I not looked in my letter box to again read that last letter of 'my vidow' as Charley called her, it really might have been her *last*, because, until she received my second letter, she thought it was *I* who had played the 'yoke', and it wasn't funny!

The next letter I wrote to 'my vidow' was on Dec. 24, 1902. I tried to send a small gift by hiding a tiny very flat nugget under Queen Victoria's stamp. This avoided a lot of red tape. The tiny gold flake nugget was worth 60 cents, which, I wrote, "the Queen is trying to hide from you." My letter was received on Jan. 17, 1903, and "the Queen came conveying the precious goldie all right," she wrote. "I prize it very much." Then comparing the high cost of all food in the Klondike with prices in the states, she continued, "Your price list of food supplies does indeed seem shocking.

"I have been very busy for a few days. I do work occasionally down town; helps out with expenses somewhat. The first year after my husband's death, I kept up all expenses by my work, as there is very little income from my few acres. I have a jersey cow, a few chickens, and a good garden and raise most all we eat, so have mostly only staple things—as flour, sugar, salt etc., to buy from the store. By careful managing last year my grocery bill was only $27. Recently I have been granted a widow's pension from the Carnegie fund, in recompense for my husband's death. This fund will allow me $10 a month for 50 months, so you see I have no need to worry, and do not have to work so hard, and have more time to be at home with my children."

Children in The Klondike

CHAPTER 15

Klondike Cabins

Here on Quartz Creek by the last of October 1902, it had begun to get quite cold, but we had laid in a good supply of provisions for the coming winter, and by November we commenced to take out the pay dirt. My part of the work was to fire the boiler, drive the points and pan the ground to have an idea of its value. Our gold pan was shallow with flaring sides 12 to 15 inches across. This we filled with some gravel to be panned and some water, then sloshed it around with a circular motion to wash out the gravel. The gold being heavier, gradually settled to the bottom of the pan in a small handful of fine gravel. We could then pick out any nuggets and procure the gold dust treasure.

That Thanksgiving day I spent in Dawson. Methodists, Catholics, Presbyterians, and the Church of England all had services on Thanksgiving day, and that night the Salvation Army had a march. The 'Army' had done a great amount of good in Dawson, I think more than the other denominations. They always had wood to cut as a job for the miners who were down and out, and fed and cared for them. Another dedicated service was by Father Judge, Catholic missionary priest, at his hospital. Father Judge helped any and all in need. In his hospital he nursed the desperate men, sick in mind and body, even through those starving times when no food could get through the ice bound passageways. He nursed them day and night with no regard for himself, until he too succumbed. At Dawson, gambling, liquor, and vice of all kinds lured many a miner to lose it, once he had got a bit of gold. It was like a fever and went to their heads, and made them recklessly fling it away after the weary boredom of darkness and dirty drudgery in the mines. People from all parts of the world were there for the lure and enticement of gold.

Back at our claim again, I was grateful to have two good men as partners and the wife of Scavdale cooked for us all and kept things in good order. At eleven o'clock in the morning it was not yet full daylight on December 22, and at two o'clock it would begin to get dark again. Although we had this dim light, we had not seen the sun itself for over a month, and then one month more of darkness and gloom before we could again welcome the sun's cheerful face. This had been a very mild winter so far; the coldest weather yet had been only 50° below zero, with only about one foot of snow.

Our cabins here were fairly comfortable. As a rule they were very warm because they were low, built of logs chinked with moss, and easy to heat. Usually there was no wind except on the high ridges and it was a dry cold. Some cabins had ground floors, some had pole floors, and others had real boards. Most all had one window, but some had no light at all. The doors were always low enough to knock one's head when we entered. Our cabin had been raised up by a spring or glacier, the which boiled up into one corner of our cabin. I jumped out of bed one morning into two inches of water, and was I surprised! I had made part of the floor out of dry goods boxes, some slabs, and about one third was open for the spring. Our chairs were boxes with board backs. Our table was made by boring two large pin holes in the logs and nailing three boards on. Our stove was made of sheet iron and weighed 20 pounds. This was the usual kind of stove found on the creeks. Our bunks were made of poles and some native hay for bedding. A good many used brush boughs of spruce trees. I had my drying pole over the stove, and my partners each had one also. These poles were seen in all cabins in the winter. This is what was on my pole, and the same on most every pole. First, one pair of moosehide moccasins, one pair of No. 12 rubber shoes, 10 pair of socks, two pair of German wool socks, and a suit of underwear.

I had my drying pole over the stove

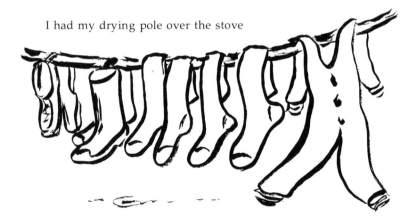

* * * * CHAPTER 16 * * * *

Inside Gold Mine, and Work

Now through your mind's eye, let us go into the tunnel. First, to picture it, you will notice these pipes that conduct the steam to the pay streak to thaw the ground. This tunnel is about 90 feet into the hill. Also notice, as we go in, that we are descending about one foot to eight. Overhead is frozen muck. Here is the pay streak. At about 100 feet perpendicular you will notice that there is a difference here. This water washed ground is 'pay'. Next to it this sharp cornered rock broken up by fine volcanic action has never been washed or worn by action of water. This gravel or wash is the dividing line or gravel of the pay which is thrown back as waste, as you see those large piles of gravel over there. See this large bone. This is the leg of a mastodon, and that one there is a tusk. Over here is the sump where we siphon out the water made by thawing the frozen ground. This here is a pan of pay dirt which I will just pan out to show you how it is done. The pan is held under the water and whirled around like this, with a swirling motion, and the gold, being the heaviest, settles on the bottom of the pan, with black sand, which is in all pay dirt. This is an average pan, about five cents. This mine is white with frost all over the inside, as it is frozen solid.

Even the inside of our cabins have cobwebs of frost all over the log walls, and outside we have learned by painful experience never in winter to touch metal of any kind with the bare skin, or we would leave a patch sticking to it. When outside, we spoke only when necessary, as the breath froze about the mouth, eyes and nose, every hair sheathed in ice. The caps have nosebands of fur to lessen danger of freezing, as the nose will freeze at 40° below and turn white. It must then be thawed by rubbing with snow before entering a cabin.

Our mail was carried 400 miles on sleds until the river opened in the spring, or about the first of June, so it took a good while for mail to come and go. The Yukon is nearly as large as the Mississippi River and much swifter. There is enough force in the Yukon to run an electric plant and more. We used wood to burn in our stoves. Spruce and birch was mostly all the kinds we had.

Returning to my duties in the mine, my work was also to siphon the water out of the mine into a tank in the boiler house,

45

From left to right in Ball, Scavdale, Anderson's Mine by candle light. Back row: Scavdale, Anderson (two neighbor miners ~ names unknown) Front row: A.E. Ball, Mr. Goyne. (the rest are neighbor miners ~ including the Hill's and their children)

and to cut the wood. My two partners would wheel the pay dirt out to the dump where it would be ready for the spring washup, which was as soon as the snow would melt in the spring and the water began to flow in the creek. I will say here that we thawed the ground by keeping about 80 to 90 pounds pressure on the steam gage on our boiler, and with the pressure of hot steam forced through the pipes into the earth in our mine, the earth was thawed.

The steam pipe was connected to a 12 foot steam hose leading to a crosshead which had five or six nipples with valves and short pieces of hose attached to steel points by clamps. These points were made mostly of old rifle and gun barrels. The valves at the crosshead were so we could turn the steam on or off as we saw fit. We would turn the steam into the points, driving them into the frozen ground slowly, with mauls made of mastodon tusks. The hot steam would soon thaw the ground. This made it possible to drive the points into the ground between the gravel and the bedrock as fast as the steam would thaw it. It generally took me about three hours to set the points full depth, or four feet. We would keep the steam on six to eight hours, during which time I sawed wood and fired the boiler, and panned to know if the amount of gold dust in the pan showed we were following the pay streak. I had to keep the ground thawed two days ahead of my partners, as the ground had to cool 40 hours before it could be taken out, on account of the hot steam.

I tunneled across the channel of the creek to get the lowest possible point for our sump, where we had our siphon pipes to get the water out of the mine and siphoned it to a tank in the boiler house to be used again. When the lowest place in the channel was obtained on bedrock, this is where the paystreak was; and when the bedrock raised three feet, was where the bench claim began, which was 35 feet above the creek claims. This was all hard work, and when I turned on the steam in the mine, the steam would bring down a rain of muddy water and mud, which was very disagreeable. I wore a long slicker coat, and the water and mud would run down over me. When I would come out of the mine with two pans of dirt to the boiler house, the intense cold would freeze the mud to the coat. I would take it off and hang it by the hot boiler while I would pan out the pans of dirt and cut some wood. Then I would go back and get two more pans of dirt, which was part of my routine of work each night for seven long months. We lit the mine with candles. When Scavdale and Anderson were wheeling the dirt out to the dump, I always carried a candle lantern which I made out of an eight inch tin can with one side cut out.

I wore a long slicker coat, and the water and mud would run down over me

CHAPTER 17

Frozen Man, and Dogs ~ Fossils in Mine

One day Mr. Goyne came down the creek and wanted us to go with him to where a man was frozen on his sled which had caught in a bush, and the man's dogs had eaten about half the flesh from his bones. We went and took the dogs which Goyne had brought home with him and fed. The man had come over the summit and was frozen, and the trail was unbroken, so the dogs got off the trail where the sled caught in some bushes, and had been there about two days. Mr. Goyne had heard the dogs barking and went to see what was the trouble. The dogs had got hungry and all then followed their instinct for self-preservation and devoured the only flesh at hand. We sent him to the morgue at Dawson where frozen men were piled up like cordwood. They found the man was from lower Dominion Creek, Dawson was about 32 miles from our place on Quartz Creek.

Along the creek one man had rheumatism so bad, he could not lie down, but could only sit doubled up in a chair. He finally died and the men had to strap his body to a board to make it straight for burial. A number of men were watching through the night until they could care for him, when all of a sudden the body sat bolt upright, breaking the straps. The men were so terrified by this eerie happening that they burst from the cabin and ran shrieking down the creek.

During our work we took out of our mine many fossils and bones of mastodons, moose, elephants, and skulls of what appeared to be water buffalo or caribou, which were very large. We found mastodon teeth that weighed 42 pounds, and one tusk quite good that weighed 250 pounds. From the tusk, I cut a 12 inch long piece from the small end that was six inches in diameter, and brought it home. I also brought a baby mastodon tooth about 3" x 5" x 9" and a larger one 6" x 9" x 12". They were molars with large roots and had broad rough grinding surfaces with deep parallel ridges. Other specimens brought home from our mine were gold dust and nuggets, some of which had quartz in them and were very beautiful. I also brought black sand which is always found where gold occurs, and perfectly faceted black diamonds (which had no intrinsic value), and deep red garnets found in granite rock. I split one granite rock which revealed the

A mastodon tusk taken from our mine weighs 250 lbs., has some 3 feet crumbled away from each end of tusk. Man in photo is 7 feet tall.

natural facets of a ¾ inch garnet still half embeded in the rock, and brought it home that way to show how they are naturally formed. I also found a number of agates beautifully streaked with yellow and orange, and some like pearl which were later appraised as of high quality when some were made into jewelry.

My greatest prize was a big gold nugget the size of a walnut; also the dozen or so smaller nuggets, each about ⅜ size which I had made into a gold nugget watch chain with a fine gold and quartz nugget fob of ½ inch size. These keepsakes included also my small brass gold scales and troy weights with which I weighed all my gold. Another item was a pair of wooden snow spectacles we had to wear to prevent snow blindness when the sun returned in the spring after three winter months of darkness. To make them we carved cup shaped wooden eyeshields, connected in one piece across the nose. Each eye cup had a narrow slit to let in less light, and the inside of each eye shield was blackened by charring with a hot poker. We also found resinous lignite coal veins in the mine, of which I kept a sample. Out of a ⅜" x 10" long piece of ivory I carved a watch chain with links within links, not cut apart, with an ivory anchor for a fob. Another item I prized was a pair of fine pale green sealskin mittens, elbow length, inside of which we wore wool mittens. All clothing had to be loose or circulation would stop, with frozen fingers or feet. Several pairs of heavy wool socks inside of moosehide moccasins kept our feet warm.

Wooden snow spectacles

51

* * * * CHAPTER 18 * * * *

Astronomy of the North

Referring to these marvels of the Klondike country and how they came to be, with the bones of prehistoric creatures clearly from a tropical zone, then frozen here, made me reason out the changes that may have caused such an enigma. Many centuries back, Greek and Roman astronomers claimed that Cynosure or the Polar Star, was the exact center of the northern hemisphere of the heavens. At about the beginning of the 19th century there was about 2½ degrees variation. About the year 1930 the latest astronomers claim there is 3⁷/₁₀ degrees, which goes to show there is a constant change taking place. This would indicate approximately one degree of change in 100 years or about 69 miles each century. This shows it would take about 9000 years to place, what is now at the Equator, at the North Pole. This is how I account for the antediluvian bone fossils so far north. Some of the large mastodon tusks have the appearance of having been bleached and cracked by the sun in a hot tropical climate for centuries before they were rotated to an arctic climate where they have been buried in the frozen ground for centuries more. This will not conflict with astronomy, or vary with the physical motion of the earth, but rather confirm it.

I was careful to observe the Aurora Borealis or Northern Lights in the far north, which has been a wonder to mankind through ages past. In the north regions these lights are more frequent.

Here I give my idea of the cause of this wonder of nature. So near the arctic circle, I seemed to be almost under this great phenomenon, and noticed that it never appeared except when a sudden change took place from warm to cold. And that occurred only when the cold currents from the south and also from the north, pressing it together on the warmer atmosphere, carried it far above the natural atmospheric belt of the earth. This was forced to such a height as to come in contact with the rays of the sun which come across the rotundity of the earth. This causes reflections similar to the reflections of the rainbow, and where these are great streamers or flashes is where the cold air is greatest, causing the warmer currents to wave or flashes to shoot upward. When the pressure of the atmosphere becomes exhausted, the flashing or shooting of the atmosphere becomes also exhausted. The brilliancy will then cease, and settle down to a steel grey, and die off first in the east. The cause of its dying off first in the east is due to the turning of the earth eastward, taking the atmosphere out of the line of the sun's rays. This may not appear very plain to persons not acquainted with astronomy and the motion of the earth, but it is about as well as I can account for it.

Mastodon skull and tusks uncovered at a depth of 42 feet on #5 below Mack's on Quartz Creek, Yukon Territory. Weight, about 1500 lbs. Took 38 men with ropes to lift to the surface. A.E. Ball helped on the ropes.

Photo of Dawson Fireman iced over after a winter fire

* * * * CHAPTER 19 * * * *

Temperatures ~ Day and Night ~ Old Cap

A picture I have shows a Dawson Fireman all covered with ice and icicles from eyes, whiskers, and moustache, after a big fire in winter time. I have been covered with ice nearly like this. We had by February 18, 1903, passed through the long dark days with the thermometer as low as 78° below zero, but soon day and night were equal, and by June 20, one was 24 hours all daylight. The weather at noon each day was quite nice and had shown signs of thawing, but through the night it got colder and by morning was down to 15° to 20° below zero again. My partners and I had arranged to have our pictures taken on the claim with our mining outfit the last of May, when even then, some snow would still be on our hillsides.

At our mine, our tunnel was now about 120 feet in to the pay streak, and when that far back under the side of the mountain, we were about 200 feet perpendicular to the outside. Our tunnel was inclined about 20 feet, which made it quite steep to wheel the dirt out of the mine. We had a large Newfoundland dog named Cap, which we hitched to the front of the wheelbarrow. He was a fine good dog to pull and was a big help. He was so big, he stood up with his paws over my shoulders. He was a dear faithful dog and slept in the boiler house where I always saw that he had plenty to eat and a good bed.

I will say here that the thermometer registered from 40° to 78° degrees below zero from the first of October to April, and was dark all the time. They were long frigid monotonous days until about the 20th of April on our creek, when the sun would make its first appearance for only about five minutes the first day. Each day then the sun was up a little longer until about the 10th of June, when it began to be light all the time for three months. The seven months of night was so depressing to all animate beings, except owls and wolves with their woeful wail, that we all were eager to see the light of the sun appear. The moon seemed to give its light as it does in the States.

I slept while Scavdale and Anderson worked. Mrs. Scavdale was a daring woman who had insisted on coming along, and cooked good meals for us all. While we were eating our dinner she often read interesting news to us from the Dawson daily paper, which cost us 25¢ for each number, a postage stamp cost us 25¢, or you could get 12 stamps for 25¢, because 25¢ was the smallest amount in circulation, and this was in gold dust. Everything was paid for in gold dust which was carried in little moosehide sacks, or 'pokes' as they were called. Every cabin and place of business had its little brass gold scales with troy weights standing on a small piece of brussels carpet. This carpet piece caught any stray flakes of 'dust' shaken out by the storekeeper's hand. In some places their hands trembled on purpose when weighing the dust, so some would spill, and in this way the storekeeper gleaned many extra dollars each week from the little carpet,— but at the expense of his conscience.

We miners worked every day, but once in a while we would have preaching, as Mr. Roper, a partner of brother Kinsley, was a preacher. He was busy on the windlass on my brother's claim till after dinner on the Sabbath, and then he would preach, but directly get on the job again. He said that it was necessary to do all we could, even if it was Sunday, on account of the cold climate.

This carpet piece caught any stray flakes of 'dust' shaken out by the storekeeper's hand

* * * * CHAPTER 20 * * * *

'Doctor' Ball ~ Goyne

I caught a severe cold and had to rest for two days, and was in bed when a man came to the door with an urgent request: "Mr. Ball, can you come with me to help old Mr. Goyne? He's ruptured himself and sent me to ask you to come." "But I can't go; you can see I'm sick myself. I'm sorry." So the man went back. But in a couple of hours he came again; this time pleading, "Do come, Ball; Goyne's in agony and very bad, and calls for you to come! I've brought a dog sled to take you." I never could bear to see a fellow being suffer without helping in some way, so when I realized the seriousness of this call, I forgot my own ills and was dressed and at his bedside in about 10 minutes. There were six or seven men there, all sitting around smoking till the air was thick with choking fumes. "You men! Quit that smoking around this sick man, and help." I commanded. "You've made his suffering worse with all this foul air, when you should have done something to help him. Are there any boards about?" "No boards—none at all," they mumbled.

They just sat dumb with no idea of what to do. Then I pitched in. I grabbed a pick, stuck it through the floor, pulled up a foot wide board, and sawed it in two in the middle. An old wool sock caught my eye. "Take this wool sock and tear it up into small pieces, you two men!" I directed. "The rest of you take the old man and lay him on the floor." Then I took the board I had sawed and some boxes and made a bed, with the foot some three feet higher than his head. "Now lay him on this bed and two of you hold his feet, and you other two hold his shoulders, while I press the rupture together and in." And it finally popped back.

After an hour he was beginning to feel much better, and showed some relief from his awful pain. Next I took the woolen sock that was torn into small bits, and put it in a saucer, all hot, and placed it over the rupture. At the end of three hours, as I was going to leave, Goyne called me to his bed and gave his hand in gratitude, "Goodbye Mr. Ball, you have saved my life." I looked around. "Now you men are to put him level in about an hour," I instructed, and heat the saucer for him, and be careful to have his belt hold it down tight into place." And so the man recovered. The news of this went up and down the creek, till the men began to call me 'Doctor Ball'. It was just using plain good common sense, and doing what was needed with whatever was at hand. My pioneer upbringing taught me this.

A.E. Ball and Mr. Goyne

CHAPTER 21

Obstetrician ~ Repaired Dam ~ Frozen Rescued

Some months later a man and women came to our boiler house to see me. They were strangers to me and spoke haltingly with evident embarassment. Finally the woman said, "My husband, Jan, he bashful. He want ask you be our doctor. We look for baby; come about month next." "But I'm not a doctor, folks!" I exclaimed. "You'd better get a real physician from Dawson." I was astounded at the implications in which this might involve me. "But *you*, we want, Doctor Ball. You cure sick man, Goyne. Help us, do!" Then visions of my own little mother flashed from the past. She was all alone in the frontier wilderness cabin when she brought me forth, and by her own inexperienced hands and prayers. Very evidently these good plain folk had no fear, and regarded birth as a natural experience common to mortals. So at their insistance, I promised to help them. "Just let me know, and come after me when the time comes. You'll get along fine."

In about three weeks Jan came running and puffing, most out of breath, and I went with him at once. On the way down I thought what a plight I was about to get into, and decided I must brace up and put on a bold face. When we arrived I warmed my hands and went to the patient and made an examination such as my doctor brother in Washington state did on several obstetrical cases when I was along. "Everything is all right and natural," I assured them; then I talked with some of the women who were there helping. In a few minutes the labor was stronger, and in about half an hour the new born gave its first cry. "What a beautiful baby girl!" chorused the women, as they busily cared for the infant and mother. "Now you women dress this child and keep it warm and it will be all right." Then I left, and all surely thought I was a doctor. The miners in the remote district had to cope with their emergencies as best they could. There were doctors in Dawson, but Dawson was 32 miles away and they charged big prices to come out to the creeks.

Again I was wanted when a black man and a man by the name of McNeal got into a squabble. McNeal knocked the black man and made him fall 20 feet down the mine shaft, and the man was taken up unconscious. I examined and did not find any broken bones, but he was unconscious for 24 hours. They sent for a doctor who arrived there on the third day, and he said there were no bones broken. He gave some medicine and his bill was $200, which McNeal had to pay, and also pay the black man for his time lost.

Another experience was in the spring of 1903. We had built a dam which had cost us over a thousand dollars. The dam got a hole and was about to be washed away. The hole was about 30 feet out. These dams were built on the ice, with long poles and moss on top of the poles, then ground on top of it all. We cut some brush and put in the holes and weighed them down with bags of sand and ground. I was wading in the ice cold water for about four hours, and when I came out I could scarcely walk. There seemed to be no feeling in my legs, and I do think I never did get fully over it. We saved the dam, but at great cost to me, as it gave me aches and pains in my old age.

At another time while going to Dawson for food supplies, I found a man half frozen on the trail. To start circulation I dragged the man some distance to a cabin, where I built a fire and rubbed snow on him till he was thawed out, so saving his life. However, the man lost his nose, ears, and some of his fingers and toes, so that he wished that he had not been rescued.

Well, to return to my mining work , we had some streaks of poor pay, and some very good. One spot was so good we could get a dollar a pan, and the highest pay was $7.60 a pan. For about a week we were making from a small place of coarse bedrock nearly $1000 a day. This is where we got the large nugget. Then we came to a small strip of ground where we scarcely got anything, and by the next July 1903, we were nearly worked out, and had taken out a total of $29,000. Our expenses were $2000, leaving about $9000 for each of us. This made me think of home so dear, and feel that it would be redeemed if I was safe home again with this hard earned product of my toil.

Canadian troops guard
the gold sacks in shipment

* * * * CHAPTER 22 * * * *

Gas in Mine ～ Three Saved ～ Canadian Award

Just at this time when I was thinking of getting ready to leave for home, I had yet another experience—the direst of all. On May 29, 1903, a man came running down the creek, calling out, "Come quick!! The men are gassed in their mine at #18 Above!" (Above Radford's Discovery). I called into the tunnel to my partners, "Bill, Charley, come quick! Some men are gassed at 18 Above!" We all started as fast as we could go, and got there most out of breath. Several men were there, all scared into a panic and afraid to go down the mine. I knew if I went down and was overcome with the the gas no one would come after me, so I thought fast and then spied a second rope lying nearby. "I'll go down, fellows, if you will do exactly as I say and help me." I grabbed the second rope and tied its one end to the windlass post at the mine, and the other end to my left leg with a half hitch around my body. The first windlass rope at the mine I would use to pull the gassed men out. "You men be very careful when you change the second rope from the post to the windlass to pull me up, so you don't let it drop, because that's my only way to get out alive!"

I got the first windlass rope and they let me down the shaft 52 feet to the mine. There I saw Aberg and fastened the rope on him, then jerked the rope for them to pull him out, which they did. The men got the rope off of Aberg and hallooed as they dropped it down again to me. I then fastened the rope to Wolf and they got him out to the surface. Then the rope that was on me, they put on the windlass and brought me out, overcome by the gas. When I came to, I was looking up at the clouds with anxious faces bending over me. I was dizzy and sick with a bad headache.

In about half an hour Aberg began to stir, and seemed conscious for a few moments. With painful effort he spoke, "There's another man in the mine," then lapsed back unconscious by spells. Aberg seemed to be deranged, and we thought he meant his partner, Mr. Wolf. When next Aberg was conscious I told them, "Raise Wolf up, so Aberg can see we got his partner out." This they did, Wolf's form still limp. But, "No!" gasped Aberg, "Another man is in the mine. It's Owen Conley from Dawson." I had seen Mr. Conley coming up the creek, and exclaimed, "Boys, he's telling us right!" And we hurried back to the mine shaft. But again no one would go down; so, even though I was still very sick, that man's life was at stake. "I'll try to go once more! We've got to get Conley out!"

So we arranged the ropes as previously. As I got on the windlass rope, they gave me four lighted candles and let me down. I went back along the tunnel about 40 feet and saw Conley. My candles were gone out, but I went to him in the dark, and putting the windlass rope around, hallooed for them to pull, then started to go to the shaft myself. However, in the darkness, I struck my head on the roof gravel of the mine, made a step or two, and that was all I knew till I was up again, and looking up at the mute but reassuring clouds. Soon I heard voices, and by a great effort I began to talk. They told me I was unconscious 15 minutes; then someone was saying, "Conley is dead." "Take me over near him," I managed to say. I wanted to check for myself and felt for his pulse. There was none. He had been in the gas too long and was very cold. They put him in a rock box and placed him where the wolves could not get at him.

When they pulled Conley out, he was dragged past and over me, which turned me about, so that the half hitch had slipped down and tightened around my knees, but could not get off further. So I was pulled out of the tunnel feet first, head down, 52 feet to the surface, and knew nothing of it. I remained so sick and dizzy that I could not walk, so the boys cut two long poles, slit the bottoms of two gunny sacks and put the poles through them for a litter, and so carried me down to my claim. This happened on a Friday and the next Sunday an inquiry was made by Mine Inspector Grant, a doctor, and Captain Rutledge of the North-west Mounted Police from Dawson. They held a post-mortem examination, so the boys hitched up the dogs and hauled me to the inquiry. Being so sick, I sat in the sled outside the door. Aberg and Wolf were very sick, and I was not much better. The doctor told me, "You ran a great chance on your own life to venture into such a dangerous place. Only the forethought with the ropes was all that saved your life." The men thawed the ground and a dug a grave on Conley's claim and buried him there.

The Mine Inspector assured me "You will surely get some reward for the great risks you took to save these men's lives. I can recommend you for a position in the Canadian Government." "But my home is in the United States," I replied, "and I wish only to return there."

While I was sitting on the sled during this inquiry, I heard a noise to the left, and looking around saw a young bear had come down from the mountainside and was pawing over and licking some meat, molasses and honey cans. He was about two thirds grown, so I hailed the men inside. "Boys, here's some bear meat for you!" But the men thought he was too fine a specimen for that. "Let's take him alive! Here's a rope." One man twirled the lasso with sure aim. "I got him! Yea, he's a fine one. Hey! hold him off while I fasten the rope round that young tree." But the bear struggled and tore off the bark and splintered that tree into kindling, and finally choked himself to death. Such is the instinct for freedom. The men butchered the cub and we had bear steaks to eat. I was sick for two weeks and more before I was fit to work.

After leaving the Klondike while visiting my sister and mother in Washington state, I had a letter from the Captain of the Northwest Mounted Police, which enclosed a gold medal from the Canadian Government. It was the size of a 25 dollar gold piece, and was inscribed for heroic services in rescuing Wolf, Aberg and Conley from the gas filled mine. Later, some three weeks after arriving at my own home, a letter came from Aberg with another letter enclosed from his mother, in which she wrote, "I would like to see the man who has saved my boy. If you are ever in need of a home, come to us here in Minnesota, and you will have a home with us as long as you live."

The Mine Windlass

CHAPTER 23

Big Nugget ~ Dawson News Articles

By June 14, 1903 our washup was nearly three times as large as we expected. In figures, we cleaned up $8816.62 for each of us. In avoirdupois, it would weigh about 50 pounds, or 49 pounds in troy weight, all gold. One night that June I dreamed that we were going to find a large nugget at a certain place when we would get there. I told my partners about my dream and proposed, "I would like to have this nugget on my share of gold when we find it." They laughed at me and bantered, "Sure you can have it, it's only a dream." But I *did* find the big nugget just where I had dreamed it was. It was the size of a walnut and worth $48.55, and was one of the treasures I brought home from my mine. From a Dawson paper at this time were the following headlines and article about it:

June 1903, Quartz Creek is a Big Producer. Discovery is Good. Oldest Claim in the Klondike Camp Producing Twice as Much from its Dumps this Year as Expected — Big Nugget Found.

Radford's Discovery; the first claim ever recorded in the present limits of what is now generally known as the Klondike Camp, is distinguishing itself this spring by producing well. The fact this claim continues to produce so many years is looked on as one of the strongest indications that placer claims in this country are not worked out and exhausted in a short time. The claim known as Radford's Discovery was staked a year or two before the famous world startling discovery was made on Bonanza Creek by George Carmack in August 1896, and Before Bob Henderson staked his discovery claim on Gold Bottom.

The largest nugget ever taken from Quartz Creek was washed out a few days ago on Radford's Discovery, and is in possession of Bill Scavdale, A.E. Ball, and Charley Anderson, the present owners of the claim. The nugget weighs $48.55. It is almost round in general shape, but has some ugly gashes in the sides, and in one place contains a little spot of quartz. Mr. Ball, who is in the city this week, has been showing the big nugget to his friends. He calls it the nest egg of the camp, because it is the biggest piece of gold from the pioneer claim. "Quartz Creek," says Mr. Ball, "is probably the richest creek of its size in the camp." It is admitted to be spotted, but it carries the gold and is producing well this season. Dumps are

"The Clean up" at #1 above Radford's Discovery, June 16, 1903, pictures (1) A.E. Ball, (2) Anderson, (3) Scavdale, partners. Also John Bergner, A.A. Johnson, and James Peterson, partners on a nearby claim. (note the cabin roof is full of bones dug from the mine)

out on all parts of the creek this spring, and claim owners are busy washing the pay dirt. From our dumps we are washing more than twice what we expected the dirt to run, and are getting fairly good pay.

Another News Item:

Original Gold Producing Creek of the Camp has out a Number of Valuable Heaps of Precious Alluvial Dirt for Spring Cleanup. (Special to the *Daily News*), Quartz Creek, April 18, 1903.

While mushing along the creek I noticed that there was never so good an outlook for the creek as at the present. Many large dumps and better pay from the miners owning them, is the report all along the creek. Commencing at 18 Above Radford's Discovery there is a good sized dump taken from a narrow paystreak. Miners are preparing for the cleanup. We have out large dumps and are expecting a rich harvest. The gold on the claim is coarse. Mr. Eckerson showed nuggets weighing $12. Work has begun on No. 11 with good pans of coarse gold. Numbers 10, 9, 8, 7, 6, 5, 4, and 3 are owned by parties who are busy operating elsewhere, and will soon be opened up.

Mr. Goyne is busy on his ground at No. 7 Above. He is working alone. He is a man of invention and has made a unique windlass. A weight balances his bucket, and he rides down with its aid, which he finds of a great help. Johnson, Peterson, and Bergner have out a large dump and will no doubt harvest a better yield than in former years. They expect to have their claim worked out the coming fall. A.E. Ball, the first man to run a long tunnel to the pay streak, has proven that the tunnel system of work is the best at this point on the creek. There are four long tunnels descending to the pay streak, and others being run, three of which are on Radford's Discovery, owned by G.P. Scavdale, Charley Anderson, and A.E. Ball, who expect to have the claim worked out this coming summer. Mr. Anderson will then commence extensive operation on his claim No. 4 Above Radford's.

Hill is running two tunnels to the pay streak on No. 6 Below. No. 3 found the largest pan of golden sand this winter, which was $28.50 and has out 19,000 buckets of pay dirt. All the claims down to *Mack's Discovery* have large dumps and are about worked out. *Fifteen* and *Sixteen* seem to be the banner claims of the creek. Yet Numbers 2 and 3 Below Mack's Discovery, owned by Sharp and Baker, have the largest dump on the creek. Good reports come from Little Blanch. Several deep holes are being sunk on Quartz Creek benches for summer work. In all Quartz will no doubt beat all previous cleanups this spring.

* * * * CHAPTER 24 * * * *

Hill's Tunnel ~ *"Ve's Reech!"* ~ *Going Home*

After I had run the first tunnel on Quartz Creek back 120 feet into the hillside to strike the original stream bed and gold on #1 Above Radford's Discovery, other miners were encouraged to do the same. One was a Swedish man named Hill on #6 Below, who was quite discouraged over his claim. However, he and his wife were not easily convinced that a tunnel, which I had urged them to start, would help. I kept encouraging him, "Run the tunnel a little farther into the hill, and you will find the gold is there." "No! No! You only fool. No goldt! Youst vork for notings," he grumbled.

One Sunday I went down to examine his tunnel, and to test pan some dirt for him. I found a few cents gold in it. "Ach! No,—he salt!" and Hill's wife nudged him in disbelief. They were sure I had 'salted' it, and all this hard work tunneling,—a fool's job. Then I showed them the next pan. "Look here,—what do you think of this! There's 7¢ to 10¢ in this—and that's good pay." Hill was still suspicious, and even when he panned some for himself with 15¢ in it, they still looked sideways at me. But when Hill's next few pans yielded 25¢ to several dollars a pan, their eyes got big with wonder. The wife started dancing about hysterical with joy, and cried out, "Heinrich! Heinrich! Ve's reech! Ve's reech!" And they were.

As the work on our claims was just being finished on Radford's Discovery, the time came to total the profits on our labors and divide the gold. Anderson, the Swede, was a good faithful partner, honest as the day was long, and he was staying on. Scavdale and wife were Norweigan, and were leaving for home. He was a good worker, and it was a great help to have had his kindly wife as our cook. We had taken out approximately $29,000, with about $2000 expenses. This netted us around $27,000, making near $9000 for each from the claim.

I was now finished with all my work on the claim, and gave everything left to my partner, Charley Anderson. I bid farewell to all on the creek that I knew, and packed everything I could in a trunk and had it sent to the boat wharf at Dawson. Then I rolled my gold sacks in a blanket, strapped it to my pack strap and started for the Gold Commissioner's office. There I had my gold

weighed and paid the duty, which was 2½ cents on the dollar. I
left my gold there until I could get a boat. I paid a royalty of $74 on
four sacks of gold dust, which was 202 ounces of dust. At Dawson I happened to run across Mr. Goyne, the old man on whom I
put the rupture back. "I'd like to go home too," he lamented,
"but I'm stranded, not even enough dust for my passage."
"Well," I cheered, "if you will go with me, I'd be glad to pay your
way to Seattle." And this he was very glad to do.

Radford's Discovery, Quartz Creek. Charles Anderson ~ owner and
operator June 16, 1903

CHAPTER 25

Visits Chief Isaacs

Having made all preparation for our home trip, I remembered my promise to Chief Isaacs to visit his town, so Goyne and I went down the river to Moosehide four miles distant, to visit his Indian village. Rev. Toitty was a missionary among the Indians there. He was from London; the Church of England his denomination. He had translated the hymns of his church into the Indian tongue, using English letters; this the old Indians talk and sing. The Indian youths talk English and sing quite well. Another missionary teacher was Benjamin F. Foltz, who treated us with much kindness and said he would ring the bell at one o'clock, at which hour about 25 Indians came. Their church was built of logs chinked and covered with moss. Roofed with poles, it was chinked and covered with earth like most Klondike cabins. At the rear of the pulpit were blackboard charts printed with the ten commandments, both in English and Indian.

The services were after the Church of England, and were rendered in the native tongue as well. Most of their translation from English was made by Archdeacon McDonald, the pioneer missionary on the McKenzie side of the Rocky Mountains. Mr. Foltz had translated the Bible and a number of gospel songs into the Indian, which he calls Montezumas. The Indians accompany their singing with a rhythmical swaying of their bodies, and sing with glowing faces.

These Indians are simple yet picturesque, rugged but friendly, and are the curiosity of the Klondike metropolis. They number about 150, and are one of the numerous small tribes that inhabit the Yukon country. They are scattered along the great river which they have patrolled and called their own for centuries. They are not treaty Indians. Mr. Foltz had been a missionary among them for several years and said that they are in sympathy with worship and naturally a religious people. They hold services in the little church regularly, and seem to have no traditions or legend lore, at least we never discovered any. Mr. Foltz came from London in 1892. The Indians trust Mr. Foltz as a father, and if he tells them that their hides or furs are worth so much, nobody can deal with them for less. One thing he can't do. He can't get them to keep clean. They have no chairs, but sit on robes and mats. They have lots of fish and meat they hunt for, then dry and smoke it until it is black. Chief Isaacs has a chair and table, also pictures of King Edward and President McKinley, which he holds high. He pointed to these pictures, patted himself on the breast and beamed, "Me King Indian!"

The North Commercial Company made the Chief a present of a trip to San Francisco and return, when President McKinley was in that city. Chief Isaacs went and it was a great revelation to him. Attired in his kingly arctic robes, the Chief was presented to the President. Mr. McKinley asked him what he thought of the United States, and he replied, "White man great! Big water. Big boat. Big cars. Big village. White man many more than Indian!"

Dawson Newspaper sketch of Moosehide Indian Chief Isaacs

On Chief Isaacs' return, they sent a boat down to Moosehide, got all the Indians aboard, and took them up to Dawson to meet their Chief. The Mounted Police, the band, and a few of the big guns were at the wharf. When the Chief walked off the boat, the cannon fired and the band struck up a lively tune, which made the Moosehides squat and shy like so many quails. The Chief was attired in white man's clothes, and the Indians did not know him. He stood on a box and made an address, and not till he began to talk to them in their native tongue did they believe that it was he. He also addressed the whites in English with great dignity: "White man great! We want to be like white man. White man good to Indian. Me big Chief. Want Indian to be good to white man." They gathered around their Chief with great joy. In their childish superstitions, they thought the whites had stolen him away and they would never see him again. I shall never forget the sight of those wild men and aged women greeting their Chieftain home. It was a heart-rending sight.

They are a tenderhearted people with strong affections. Yet in earlier days—and only nine years ago—three Indians were hung at Dawson for the murder of a white man. They opened the body and filled it with stones and sunk it in the river. But the Indians have now become quite civilized. The Government does not allow anyone to sell liquor to the Indians. That must be saved for the Christian whites! Dawson was a city of 8000 or 9000 in 1903, with 30 licensed drink shops to help people be good. Dawson was larger in 1897 and '98 when more gold was being taken out than later. Bonanza and Eldorado Creeks were the richest in the Klondike country, but they were well worked out by 1903.

While on this visit to Chief Isaacs, I asked him, "Chief, what was the best thing you saw on your trip to San Francisco?" His reply was enthusiastic. "Big village! Big water! Big boat! Cars! 'Boston man' many as Chief Isaacs' brush! No moose! No caribou!" And so on, but all said in great earnestness. "Isaacs go London! See King! Next." His braves look up to him as a great man, but the tribe is fast passing away. Chief Isaacs was very pleased I had come to visit him and showed me his treasures. He had many fur pieces,—beautiful pelts—and richly beaded garments made by his people, including moccasins made of moosehide. One very prettily fashioned pair of baby moccasins made of soft chamois skin took my eye. It was all fringed and beaded, and I bought this pair in hopes I might one day have a little son to wear them. When I went to leave, Chief Isaacs insisted that I have a gift to remember him by, so from his fishing supplies he selected a four foot long sinew from a moose's leg. "You take. Make you good fish line." Their method of fishing was to chop a hole in the ice on the river and let down several feet of fishline like this with bait, then pull out the fish. And so we said farewell and returned to Dawson for our boat home.

We took the new railway 110 miles to Skagway

"Soapy Smith"

CHAPTER 26

Dawson to Whitehorse ~ Skagway
~ Entertains Royalty

At Dawson we found another younger man waiting to go, so I proposed, "Let's all get a three bunk stateroom on the boat, and we can be our own guards for our gold, and so won't have to get it insured. What we save by not insuring the gold will pay for the stateroom." "Yea man, that's a deal," they chorused. We started July 30, 1903, on the steamboat *Dawson* to sail back up the Yukon to Whitehorse. Our stateroom was eight feet square with one bunk above the other. I took the upper bunk, the young man the middle bunk, and Mr. Goyne the lower bunk. All the gold was on the upper bunk, and someone was always to be on guard with the gold. When I was out, the other two were in, and when they were out, then I was in. The ones out always locked the others in. The ticket from Dawson to Skagway cost $70, which was high. We were 12 days going from Dawson to Seattle, and the trip was a very interesting one.

The moss seemed as a green carpet stretched over the hills and valley. Higher up in the hills were trees of green and golden hues, and the mountains topped with ice and snow. In the distance to the right was the volcanic burning mountain of St. Elias. On August 2 we got to Whitehorse, 480 miles from Dawson, and took the new railroad 110 miles to Skagway. This was a far cry from the back breaking pack over Chilkoot Pass three years before.

When we arrived at Skagway, we put our gold in a bank there, as we had to wait three days to get a ship for Seattle, and had time to see the town. While we were there the Army was marching two men who had deserted and were about to be shot. They first disgraced them, made them put on civilian clothes, and took them to what was called Reid's Falls, and shot them there.

After this we visited Reid's Falls which was three miles from Skagway, up the Skagway river. The Falls were back in a narrow canyon with perpendicular walls of rock some 60 feet apart, and the trees and spray made the approach to the Falls quite dark, but we saw the Falls in their beauty. While we were standing before the Falls, it first came to me that we were again back on United

States territory, and we all began to sing *America* as loud as we could sing, and each one beat the time. When we came to the stanza, "I love thy rocks and rills, Thy woods and templed hills", Mr. Goyne broke down, and we could not sing any more. We were all glad to again realize we were on our country's soil.

The Falls were small but very beautiful, and about 60 feet high. Close by is the cemetery where Frank H. Reid is buried. A large monument marks his tomb. He was one of a Vigilante Committee organized to rid the town of Skagway of 'Soapy' Smith and his gang of outlaws, who preyed not only on the returning Klondikers, but the incoming 'Cheechako' as well. Reid shot 'Soapy' dead on the spot, and 'Soapy' shot Reid at the same time. Reid died over a week later, but the Vigilantes captured the whole Smith gang and brought them to justice. The people erected this monument for Reid's daring deed in which he lost his own life. Close by the Falls which are named in Reid's memory, is the old cemetery where both 'Soapy' Smith and Reid are buried.

Skagway is the metropolis or gateway to the overland route to Whitehorse, Dawson, and the Klondike gold fields, and was in 1903 a town of 2000. When the time came we got our tickets ($30 Skagway to Seattle) on the steamer, *City of Topeka*, and our stateroom was No. 8. As before, we had bunks together and guarded our gold safe in our first class cabin room, and felt that this land of ice and snow was soon to be seen no more, and we would shortly be with our people at home. On August 6 we arrived at the Rodman's Quartz mines. Many fish were here. Arrived at Sitka at 7 P.M. We locked the state room and I always kept the keys if I was out on deck watching the sights.

On shipboard August 7 while pacing the deck, I happened to be near a large woman finely dressed, who seemed to have several servant girls along. She asked me some questions about the great Muir Glacier and if I lived in Alaska. I saw she was an unusual person, and told her I had spent three years in the gold fields of the Klondike. I then showed her a small bag of nuggets and she seemed very much interested and spoke with longing. "I would like one to take home as a souvenir." She fancied those nuggets and appeared to be used to getting whatever she desired. I then inquired of her, "And where might your home be?" Drawing herself up to her full regal height her answer further fascinated me, "I was once the Queen of Hawaii." (Liliuokalani reigned from 1881 to 1893) and that is my home!" With a deep bow, I addressed her as only a queen should be addressed, "Your Majesty, I am deeply honored to meet you and have you choose one of my nuggets."

She examined them and selected one worth about five dollars, then invited, "Come with me to my stateroom so I can pay you and show you some of my souvenirs I have bought." I followed along with her train, and saw her exquisite array of jewelry, including some beautiful earrings, but amongst it all one thing specially caught my eye. It was a carved pearl shell penholder with a gold pen which I greatly admired. Her Majesty saw my interest. "You like my pen. I like your gold nugget. If you like pen instead of money, we trade even." So I chose the beautiful pen and was proud to take it to my mother as a gift when I saw her at Seattle. After Mother's passing it was sent back to me.

When I returned to my stateroom, my partners were agog over my tale of meeting the Queen and complained, "You get all the breaks! You stay here and let us take a look at Her Majesty today." So I chuckled, "You'll only have to be as impudent as I was and watch for a look at her and her waiters!" So they went on deck that morning, but never the Queen appeared and they came back with glum faces. That afternoon however, when I was out, she came with two of her ladies-in-waiting and began to talk, so proud of her nugget. So I contrived to give my partners the surprise of their lives. "If you would like to come to my stateroom, Your Majesty, I will show you my sacks of gold dust." "So pleased to do so," she agreed, and followed me. "The sacks are sealed," I explained, "but I can let you lift them." So I led the procession to our state room door and ushered in the Queen! My partners were so surprised they could scarcely speak. I had them hand down the gold sacks for the Queen to lift, and she almost let one drop, not knowing how heavy it was. That was one way to entertain royalty.

On August 8 we passed through Millbank Sound, and August 9 through Queen Charlotte's Sound. On August 10 we sailed through The Narrows. We were coming into the port at Victoria, Vancouver Island, and here we bade farewell to Her ex-Majesty and retinue who landed to take ship for their home in Hawaii.

A carved pearl shell penholder

CHAPTER 27

Seattle Assay Office ~ Visits Mother and Family ~ Angelina Seattle

On August 11, 1903 at 9 A.M. we arrived safely at Seattle and took our gold to the Assay Office. Here the gold dust was taken from my sacks, weighed, and exchanged for bills and gold and silver coins. One sack weighed in at $1,790 in gold dust; one had $2,964 in the sack; another $3,480 in dust; and one had $280 all in nuggets, making a total of $8,514 in value. About a year or so later at home, I received some important Government papers to sign, verifying the amounts of gold I had turned in to the Seattle Assay Office. I found the papers entitled me to a certain percentage more money—a worth while sum—with this explanation: An employee of the Assay Office who weighed the gold dust had systematically cheated the Klondikers by having places inside his shirt cuffs where he secreted some of all the dust he handled; but the truth will out, and he was caught and sentenced for embezzlement.

Here in Seattle I was glad to be with my people again. My sister Florence Jennings and family lived at Mountain View, Washington at this time. Mother lived with her, but when I arrived, Mother was away at a camp meeting. I greeted her there with tears of joy and stayed with them for three months after visiting my brothers nearby. H. Kinsley Ball, who had been in the Klondike with me, was a real estate broker in Seattle; Dr. Robert O. Ball was in his practice at Tacoma, Washington, and Dr. Judson O. Ball was a dentist and surgeon practicing in both Sioux City, Iowa, and Seattle.

At about this time Seattle was celebrating its Semicentennial, having been founded in 1852, and named in honor of a friendly Indian Chief whose name was Seattle. In 1856 some neighboring Indians under Chief Leshi assembled at Lake Washington and plotted a massacre of all the whites on the Puget Sound. However Chief Seattle and his daughter Angelina warned the settlers when she galloped horseback over the settlement to tell them of the danger. A battle was fought on the shores of Lake Washington which is now called Leshi Park. There is a boulevard started here which will be 140 miles long when finished. The United States Government is making a canal from the salt water to this lake, (which is fresh water). This is for the war and navy vessels. Angelina Seattle is buried in Lakeview Cemetery with a small natural granite monument. This marks the little unowned corner of land where she lies who saved the lives of so many from a sad fate.

At the time of the Semicentennial, Angelina Seattle still lived, and with her Indian neighbors, sold fish to the townspeople. To honor her the city presented her with a beautiful silk dress and had her ride in the parade. The next day this humble woman appeared on the streets, barefoot as usual, with her gorgeous silk dress caught up, filled with fish, and happily peddled them as was her custom. But for all the kindly warning given by this simple-hearted woman in 1856, Seattle in all its greatness never might have been.

1922 Ball Reunion Family Picture taken at the Old Homestead: Judson, Entheus, Elizabeth, Kinsley, Charley.

* * * * CHAPTER 28 * * * *

Enroute Home ~ Arrested

While in the West, my dentist brother Judson fixed my teeth, badly in need of filling. He used some of my gold to make caps for several front teeth at a total cost of $10.45. The time now came when I must leave and travel homeward, so bidding my mother and all my family good-bye, I took the train to Snohomish, Washington on Monday morning, Nov. 22 and started east. I had to stop in St. Paul, Minnesota to change cars, and waited four hours there on Thanksgiving Day. During this wait at St. Paul, I felt I must be very watchful of my belongings because I had all my three years' hard earned money in a money belt on me, and this guarded watchfulness may have made an officer suspicious of me. At any rate he tapped me on the shoulder and said I was under arrest. My new gold filled teeth had made a plausible case of mistaken identity. The officer was sure I was an escaped felon for whom there was a man hunt. The only way I could convince him was to demand that he telephone my dentist brother to establish my innocence, which he finally did, and apologized.

Leaving St. Paul at 9:30 P.M. I travelled to Chicago, and left there at 10 P.M. Nov. 25, Thanksgiving night. Now nearly home, I got to New Castle, Pennsylvania, Friday evening Nov. 26, where I had a cousin, Daisy Clark Hudson. Continuing on Saturday, I visited my brother, Prof. Charles F. Ball, Principal of Volant College. Monday I got to Mercer County and went to see brother Ellsworth's family, finally arriving Tuesday at the dear home farm I loved so well.

Everything about the old home seemed to greet me with a glad "Hello." My old team of horses seemed to know me, and I felt as a boy again as I looked over the fields and the trees that I had planted. It seemed that I was greeted everywhere by the neighbors who had bade me farewell and did not expect to see me again. They came in from all sides and I had to tell the story of the land of the midnight sun, and the land of ice and snow; and not until the late hours of night did I get a rest, so glad were they all to see me.

CHAPTER 29

Welcome Home ~ Pays Debts ~ Spring Flood ~ Has Home ~ Plants Trees

My cousin Ethel and her husband, Charley Taylor, who had rented the farm from me while I was gone, now had bought land of their own. They wanted to move on it the next April, so while I lived with them over the winter many plans were emerging to stock and fit the farm to again be my home. I had already used most of my money to pay off all my debts, and especially my debt to the elderly man who had loaned me the money for outfit and travel to the Klondike. He gripped me by both hands. "I knew you'd make it, boy! I knew you'd make it! Good lad!" "But only because of your kindness, sir, and trust that I'd return." I smiled my appreciation, opened my wallet and paid my debt, but the interest I paid in gold.

Our small town at that time had no bank, so when I first got home I decided to do as my pioneer forbears had done, and hide what was left of my money in a safe place about the house. It was now mostly in bills, so I sealed it in a Mason jar and buried it in the earth floor of the cellar, beside the spring drain which emptied into a big tile at the wall and flowed on down underground to the pasture stream. What I had not considered was that the spring rains usually raised the spring so high that it gushed from its three inch pipe like a fire hydrant, and flooded the cellar drain until water was 18 inches deep all over the cellar floor. The 18 inch tile drain was inadequate to carry the flooded spring, and so almost ended my struggles in disaster.

I was away when the rains came on and when I got home, I made a frantic check on my precious hidden jar. Woe was me! It was hidden no longer, but washed out of its earthen hole and was bobbing about on the water dangerously near the large open tile which had only a few widely spaced bars to shield it, and that might have carried the jar down to the creek.

I soon used all the money to prepare for farming again. I bought all new machinery, but still had some of my cows I had left on the place, also some sheep and pigs. In the spring Taylors moved and I was about to be left alone, but not for long. The neighbor who was widowed while I was away became my wife and homekeeper on June 8, 1904, so at last I had a home once

79

more.

Everything seemed to do well on the farm, and as father used to say, "Dilligence will prosper with bountiful crops, where indolence will fail." On October 29, 1905 our son Amos Walton Ball was born, and brought much joy. We were surely thankful to the giver of life with blessings from all sides. My ambition was to improve the old home. To commemorate this event, I planted a small field near the orchard with chestnuts, acorns, walnuts, and all kinds of tree seeds that spring of 1905. All grew well and after 25 years a small woods was doing fine.

This homestead is one of the few remaining that has been in the original owners hands·since the Revolution. This farmland was part of Lot No. 671 of 212 acres patented to my great uncle Daniel Murray in 1786 for services in the Revolutionary War. I planted the maple grove just south of the family graveyard, and because of the many springs, I brought several together and formed the little pond with its boat, and built a rustic bridge for all to enjoy. This place is hallowed to the memory of those who have gone before. Over the years I have planted several acres to maple, oak, walnut and pine, and many other trees, that it may continue to be beautiful and useful, and enjoyed by all who may call to see. Thus may we all live to make others happy and protect the beauties of nature by which it glorifies God.

I have also preserved some of the relics of bygone days, that have been of great use in their time. Sturdy chairs, walnut and cherry drop leaf tables, a high secretary desk of solid walnut, a large oak chest, a small horsehide covered trunk with rounded top, oval picture frames, and some square with carved maple leaves at corners; ox yokes, maple sap buckets, a wooden reaping cradle, and an old farm wagon—all these made by my forebears' own hands.

Preserved also I have Father's surveying instruments, many books, histories, and early writings from pioneer days. These include letters to my grandfather, Rev. Amos Ball, from former Governor William Bigler, asking him to care for the comfort of Governor Bigler's mother, who lived in a cabin at the north edge of the farm. All these and many other things that are still useful help us to recall how different our forefathers lived, and mindful of their honest pioneer ways.

CHAPTER 30

Home Rewards Labors ~ Ball Coat of Arms

This home place is surely fair to see. In all my travels I have never seen any better place adapted for a home to dwell in than here. We are in the center 'twixt great cities and rivers of renoun. Schools, churches and commerce on all sides. What more can the mind of man desire? What choicer blessing could nature build or bestow? Now nearing my four score years and sitting before my window this Thanksgiving day in my home, I can truly say I have never seen a more beautiful little valley than the one before my eyes. Though it is late fall, the fields are robed in dark green. The fields of corn and grain are gathered into the farmers' golden hoard, the cows are grazing in the valley along the meandering stream, where the boys fish and bathe during the sunny days of summer. There is no waste land. The railroad with its ponderous loads of freight of all kinds go rolling by; the aeroplanes go sweeping overhead with our slated roofs as landmarks along their aerial course. Surely this is a land blest with nature's richest treasure. May we all be thankful and steadfastly content to hold our place on this good domain.

Long since our kin chose out this lovely valley with its even slopes and gurgling springs. The ever diligent hand of industry has made this a good place to dwell, and may no ill o'ertake or cause a pang of pain, if soon we should have to part. We feel we have done our part, and have not toiled in vain, but have joy to know that we can retire, and bestow to others the blessings of our toils. Will my son be careful to hold and enjoy, and be ever careful to maintain and guard well the honor of the past? Be careful of the soil. It has been a true friend according to the amount of love and care bestowed upon it. The owner of the soil must love it. This home is full of memories past. It is rich with the lives of our association with good parentage for more than six generations here. The advantage of their labors has also been blest with good neighbors, which is a blessing to be held in high esteem. Experience teaches a good school, but it is far too expensive for the learner to risk. It is far better to use prudence, care, and good judgment, which is sometimes called 'horse sense'; it is a far safer rule to guide us to success. In conclusion, I will say to the readers of this little book: be thoughtful, do right, and you will not drift beyond nature's loving care.

"Where springs gush forth,
And trees abound,
And birds give vent
To joyous sound."

—Amos Entheus Ball

THE BALL COAT OF ARMS

REV. ROBERT BALL preached for the King. See the *COAT OF ARMS* assigned by Sir William Segangarten December 22, 1613, Book page 171, London, England, heraldry assigned to Rev. Richard or Robert Ball, the same as assigned to Lawrence Ball, except for the Latin motto. *COAT OF ARMS explanation:* The silver shield or argent of the second color cut off by horizontal lines is called the *chief* and is given for noted and honorable deeds. The demi-lion rising above the clouds signifies acts of bravery, dignity and royalty. The lion is holding a globe or *ball* and is suggestive of the name *BALL. Lion* is the king of beasts and is the charge of royalty. The *clouds* mean great difficulties overcome by rising above them. The *stars* suggest celestial figures. Hence the *motto:* "Coelum qui Tueri" — "Looking Heavenward."

* * * * CHAPTER 31 * * * *

This I believe ~ An Appreciation
—by Morgan Barnes

NOTE: A. E. BALL had a deeply religious parentage, and although he never aligned himself with any one denomination, he tried to appreciate the good in all. The following are excerpts of what he believed and lived by, written in his later years about 1930–1936:

"Nature, Spirit, God, all are invisible to mortals, yet we are dependent on them every moment. The pure in mind may see God. The evil-minded will shun to come into the presence of God, and will weep with great sorrow. No matter if I stand alone, this mind will reap where it has strewn. I have shed tears of sorrow, and tears of joy; all were satisfying to me. May my passing be calm, knowing I have been careful not to deceive myself, but jealous to have the approval of Nature's loving care. I hope it will be well with me, and hope all mankind may be equally blest, and all my near and dear ones enjoy the fullness of God's love and care. Nature cares for us day by day. Do we appreciate His loving kindness? Let us carefully think of our relation to the laws of Nature. We are as infants at our mother's breast. Let me ever think to hallow myself, and pause, before I speak the name of God. Nature is the law of God."

AN APPRECIATION OF AMOS ENTHEUS BALL

Written by the Mercer County historian, Morgan Barnes of Grove City, Pa. and published in The Mercer Dispatch, October 15, 1936.

When AMOS ENTHEUS BALL was laid to rest last Friday beside his fathers in the historic family plot among the evergreens on his ancestral farmstead, there passed from among us a remarkable personality. Properly proud of his heritage, daringly adventurous always in spirit, lover of trees and expert in all pertaining to them, lifelong collector of interesting personal and material memorabilia, serious student of economic trends, and often over-spoken in the expression of strongly held convictions, he was a man well worth knowing. In Thoreau's phrase, he kept step to the music he heard, let others march as they might. Touchstone, a few weeks ago had the memorable privilege of accompanying him on the last visit he ever made to the famous arboretum which he had planted and tended with such devoted interest. Now, after life's fitful fever, he sleeps among his kin in the shadow of the trees he loved so well, at peace in a casket made by his own hand and in a grave marked by a simple stone of his own carving. He lived a life filled with absorbing interests and his memory abides.

1900~1903

Amos Entheus Ball

The "Spring Run" at the Ball Homestead, sketched by the author as a young girl on the farm. The page, yellowed by time was from her sketchbook of 1917.

Your Majesty, I will show you my sacks of gold dust.

F. D. Moon, - Greenville, Pa.

Amos Watton Ball

father of
Amos Entheus Ball

Father had taught me to plow at 10

Preserved also I have Father's surveying instruments, many
books, histories, and early writings from pioneer days.

But at 17 I did the work of a man and helped Father make the brick and build our new ten room house in 1875. (Photo taken about 1922)

A. E. Ball (1930) holds Mastodon Tooth from Mine. Piece of Ivory Tusk (upright) rests on section of locust post being made when the news came that Lincoln was shot. Post in constant use 75 years, 1865–1930.

June, 1935—A. E. Ball with Johnny Appleseed Tree. Planted about the year 1822 by John Chapman. It bore Greening Apples till about 1970. It then was uprooted when blown down by a heavy windstorm.

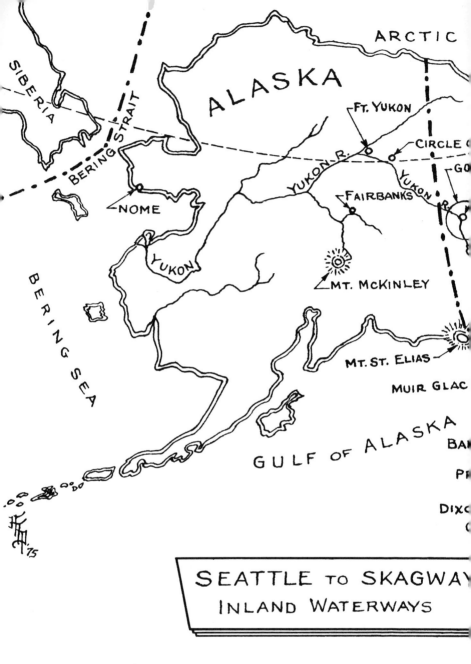

SEATTLE to SKAGWAY
INLAND WATERWAYS